Akvavit

Ak
va
vit

Rediscovering a Nordic Spirit

Rasmus Poulsgaard &
Sune Risum-Urth

Thanks & About the Authors

Acknowledgements

This book is very much a result of a collaborative effort. It started out as being an introduction book into the wonders of akvavit written for bartenders by Sune and Rasmus, but turned out to be much more than that.

We couldn't have written this book without the help of fantastic inspiring people that we met on our akvavit journey. They provided us with the inspiration, knowledge and sometimes even funding to create what we wanted. An independent book for drink nerds by drink nerds, that gives an honest peak into the Scandinavian world of flavours. A direction for a new Scandinavian drinking culture.

Søren Espersen who helped us tremendously understanding the botanical and cultural history of the akvavit botanicals. He is a true outdoor guy and we felt very inspired listening to his accounts of uncultivated caraway and the flavours of the wild. We are certain there is an entire book hidden in there somewhere.

Lars Kragelund. Where to start? He was the first guy we met when we started our akvavit journey 4-5 years ago. Lars is an inextinguishable fountain of knowledge that we leached onto like piglets on a teat. His passion and drive for the category is unrivalled and we couldn't have done it without him.

Arcus, the company Lars represents, provided us with support financially. Their fiscal aid, given without strings attached, is what made this book possible. For that, we are grateful.

All the bartenders who not only took the time to engage in discussions on akvavit, but also inspired us to change direction half way through the process. This book is for you, and it is you alone who can change and shape the idea, people have about akvavit.

Bjørn Ortmann is the guy who designed the visual identity of the book. Thank you for listening and helping us realize and visualize our dream.

Matilde Digmann works wonders with brush and ink, and her work with the illustrations made the pages come alive. We are grateful for her patience and talent.

Just reading the whole book is something of an effort and deserves praise, let alone proof reading it. William Bjarnø did just that and if you find a comma or syntax error please report them to our special hotline 1-800-TELLSOMEONEWHOCARES.

Rasmus haven't taken all the pictures in this book, but most of them. We tried to capture as many of them as possible, but the timing of our visits sometimes made it impossible to take ambience pictures of the bars we visited. We would like to thank all the bars, and the hotel, for providing us with pictures, so we were able to give our readers a glimpse into the magic of the bars we visited.

The Authors

Sune Risum-Urth and Rasmus Poulsgaard met each other in 2009 at Copenhagen based cocktail bar Ruby, where they both worked for 5 years, 4 of them together. It was a pioneering time when the Danish cocktail culture as we know it today was in its formative years, and at one point the couple stumbled upon akvavit.

It wasn't love at first sight, but it was definitely an epiphany that suddenly made sense on so many levels for us as bartenders in Denmark. For most Scandinavian people akvavit is somewhat stigmatized, as our main encounter with it is through throwing back 20+ shots of ice cold akvavit at several Christmas lunches a year. Something that

would make most people develop a somewhat strained relationship with any spirit.

Nick Kobbernagel-Hovind, who is bar managing Ruby and feature in this book was invited along with Rasmus to Manhattan Cocktail Classics in 2013 to do a seminar as representatives of the Scandinavian cocktail culture. At the time, akvavit was not something they had used that much because of the previously described stigmatization, but faced with the prospect of having to speak about something that was specifically Scandinavian they dove into the world of akvavit totally unaware of the journey that it would take them on.

Sune joined the project with a vengeance a bit later and has now even gone into producing akvavit at his full-time occupation as a distiller at Copenhagen Distillery. Rasmus also moved on from Ruby and does a lot of freelance work; cocktail photography, seminars etc. Along with Kasper Riewe, who also feature in this book, they have created their own artisanal cachaça brand called "Fio do Bigode".

Together Sune and Rasmus have traveled and educated bartenders in Scandinavia on the wonders of akvavit in cocktails to the point where they just had to write a book.

Indholdsfortegnelse

5	Acknowledgements	89	NEW YORK — fall 2016
6	The Authors	89	Nomad
		94	Mace
10	Beet root basher	100	Up&Up
	Cocktail break		

12 A HISTORY OF AKVAVIT

20 Stress Reliever
Cocktail Break

22 WHAT IS AKVAVIT?

30 Caraway and Chocolate
Cocktail Break

40 A Martini
Cocktail Break

42 A TALE OF TWO DISTILLERIES

44 Nordisk Brænderi and VI.ER AKVAVIT

55 Aalborg Nordguld Akvavit and Lars Kragelund

64 The Nordic Negroni
Cocktail Break

66 AKVAVIT ABROAD

69 LONDON — summer 2016
69 Original Sin
76 White Lyan
84 Calloch Callay

89 NEW YORK — fall 2016
89 Nomad
94 Mace
100 Up&Up

106 AKVAVIT AT HOME

108 SWEDEN — winter 2016/17
108 Hay Market
114 Open/Close
126 Familjen

134 NORWAY — winter 2016/17
134 Raus
142 No Stress
150 Pigalle

158 DENMARK — spring 2017
158 Skt Pauls Apothek
166 Duck and Cover
174 Ruby

184 MIXING A SCANDINAVIAN IDENTITY

189 Akvavit and Flavour Harmonies
192 Flavourmap

194 Akvavit Læsk
Cocktail Break

196 Old Techniques for New Cocktails

212 That's all folks

Beet root basher

BY RASMUS POULSGAARD

Root vegetables or just roots in general and akvavit is one of the greatest revelations in my journey in mixing with akvavit. It just works every time. Later I found out a lot of the root vegetables are either in the same botanical family or rather closely related with the akvavit botanicals, but not all of them – and they still work!

It is a dark, spicy and savoury cocktail, but still quite light and vibrant on the palate. A very different cocktail experience indeed, but when serving it at the Duck and Cover I was surprised how easy people bought into the serve. Everybody just seemed to like it!

For one drink

6 cl Dill akvavit
Juice of 1/2 a lemon
1 pinch of celery salt
1 bar spoon simple syrup
4 cl beetroot juice
4 cl ginger beer

Garnish with salted beetroot crisp or sliced beet root, a slice of ginger and a dill sprig.

A

y of

akva

1

History

avit

A brief history

The evolution from coarse out house hooch in the late 1600s to the clean and professional product of the late 1800s is a fascinating tale. And it is a journey that almost every spirit in the world has gone through.

From the time we realized fermented sugar made us dizzy, we, as a species, have been on a steadfast journey to perfect the buzz. The flavoured spirits like genever, gin and akvavit are splendid examples of this, as the idea of flavouring spirit with botanicals is as old as the process of distillation itself. We shall explain;

The early idea about spirit was that it was the etherical fifth element sought after by alchemists. We had Fire, Water, Earth and Air, but Ether was thought to be the last piece to the puzzle. Not ether as in "cloth-to-mouth-pulling-people-into-vans" ether, though it has its name from the same idea. But the essence of the ethereal. The discovery of the liquid that came out of condensing the vapours of boiled wine was a scientific breakthrough that would change the course of history. Most important for the discovery was the quick realization that alcohol would very readily take flavour from anything submerged in it.

This led to the logic conclusion that medicinal properties would be absorbed as well, and thus a new type of medicine was born. So juniper is good for inflammation in the liver, you say? We shall make an extract of it to help cure you. Would you like the courage of a bear? Why not soak a bear's heart in alcohol and drink the liquid? With modern eyes the theory has some apparent flaws, but to judge history by modern standards is to try and make your way across Manhattan with a map of London.

We find that the herbs used in local spirits tend to reflect local culture. Gin is a good example – exotic spices from

> "This led to the logic conclusion that medicinal properties would be absorbed as well, and thus a new type of medicine was born."

all around the world was shipped to London by the merchant fleet and the sailors were used to the flavours. It comes as no surprise that all these exotic spices ended up being used to mask the putrid smell of dock side distillation. In Scandinavia, the picture is slightly different. We get some spices from the Hansa fleet, but the plants used in akvavit mainly come from the monastery gardens from whence they spread and became household herbs.

Anis, dill and fennel are all found spread wide across Scandinavia since the 14-1500s. They are imported from the Mediterranean region for a range of medicinal purposes; antiseptic, purifying, as a stimulant or to calm you down, for lack of sexual prowess or excess of same, for curing fever, bad temper, gas and a very large number of other ailments.

Caraway has the jury out debating still. We find microfossils in gardens all the way back to the early 1200s, but also evidence of gathering of wild caraway predating that. Whether it is indigenous to Scandinavia will blow in the wind, but with about 1000 years of history we will gladly claim it as our own. It is used for more or less the same ailments as the others, only its high concentration of carvone gives it a very distinct profile that stands out from the quite anise-y outline of the other three.

But for hundreds of years, alcohol was thus a medicine – and more than that: a luxury commodity reserved for the upper class. But slowly alcohol became more and more normal. We back track a bit here;

In 1405 in "the Annals of ClonmacNoise" we find the word uisce beatha, as a direct translation into Irish gaelic of 'aqua vitae'. That becomes "whisky". At the same time, the French were already making eau de vie, which is, of course, French for aqua vitae. The shortened "aquavit" appears in 1506 in a letter to the arch bishop of Trondheim from the Danish emissary Eske Bille. He offers a bottle of it as a "remedy to all ailments within and without". The gift wasn't, however, a remedy against Norway's objection to being a Danish protectorate, and Eske spends a large part of his vocation as a prisoner.

Still in the early 1500s, the first distillers to settle in Scandinavia were weapons manufacturers, or more specifically, powder makers. Denmark could secure sufficient amounts of gunpowder from Germany. Sweden and Norway did not have this option and therefore had to learn how to make their own. Alcohol was used as a lubricant in the process of grinding the raw materials without lessening their flammability. This may seem like a bad idea in hindsight, but

On a Side Note

Around the same time, an Anna of Denmark was married away to the arch duke of Sachsen. She was renowned for her recipes for akvavit which she would send to other noble houses whenever she heard someone was sick. At her death, she allegedly took close to 200 individual recipes to her grave. 5 generations later her direct bloodline ascended the throne of England in the shape of William of Orange, who brought the technology needed for distilling on grain to England, from where it quickly spread to the rest of the north and thus the gin craze of the British Isles and the Great Scandinavian Intoxication could begin. All is connected, all is intertwined.

it worked and made killing other people a whole lot easier. We should mention that Scandinavia has a very long and proud tradition of being at war with itself, when we weren't busy beating up England or the other way around.

Household Hooch

In the late 1600s one in a hundred households in Denmark had a still in their outhouse. That is approximately one for each parish. By the mid-1700s that number had exploded to one in three. It was a common thing to have a still in the part of the house that we still call the "bryggers" – or the "brewery" – where you would, surprisingly, make your beer too. The alcohol produced was dangerous on a good day. Lead was commonly used to make the metal parts of the still more malleable, zinc and other polluting agents where plentiful. Furthermore, the process behind the distillation was a complete mystery. A man's courage was measured by the first drops to come out of his still, basically the part we today avoid at all costs, as it contains a whole fist full of harmful compounds.

But with the spread of technology, the purpose changed. Akvavit was no longer primarily a medicine, but had become the favoured recreational drug of the masses. The art of adding botanicals changed then, from a medicinal purpose to a matter of hiding the bad taste of hastened or impatient distillation. Livers where failing, noses where reddening, society was falling apart.

From the mid-1600s a sort of arms race began between governments and producers. One side wished to limit the harmful effects on society, while the other sought to make a living. The English Gin Act (mid 1700) is an example of this as is the Norwegian rule that there can only be one distillery per parish (in effect mid 1600). In Denmark, peasants

> "The flavouring returns as a matter of enjoyment and taste, rather than a necessity born from bad craftsmanship."

were forced under threat of imprisonment to leave towns before noon out of fear they would squander their earnings on drink.

Alongside these attempts to limit the access to alcohol another development took place. The craftsmen sitting by their stills slowly taught themselves how their machines worked, and in 1810 the first Danish school for distillers was founded in Copenhagen. From then on, distilling was a licensed profession. The continuous still was born in the early 19th century and later patented in a variation by Henry Coffey.

From Pernod in France over Plymouth in England to Isidor Henius' Taffel Akvavit from 1846, the fashion became to advertise the purity of the product. The spirit today known as Absolut was originally called "Absolut Renat Brennevin" – meaning completely purified burned wine – and old bottles, or new bottles with old labels, of spirit from Northern Europe can still be found to advertise their content as "fusel free". The flavouring returns as a matter of enjoyment and taste, rather than a necessity born from bad craftsmanship.

The history of spirit in Europe is a tangled web of thorny vines. Go back far enough in history and the divisions fall apart. There is no Danish or English history without the influence from Holland, Germany or France. There is no American history without the European colonies, no rum without sugar, no sugar without slaves. We will, however, go so far as to admit there is a specific sentiment about alcohol in the north. We flavour it. Genever, gin and akvavit originate from the same idea, the same background. Even whisky used to be flavoured – the main reason it isn't flavoured today, is out of spite and to annoy the English who imposed a tax on flavoured spirits.

But as time passed subtle regional differences became national traditions and today we all believe that we drink as we drank since time immemorial. The reality is much more complex. Random influences have created our current culture, the historical causalities are shrouded in evolutionary coincidence and when we go back in history everything seems to melt together with no clear distinctions.

But still, today there ARE differences, arbitrary as they may be. And as we intend to demonstrate in the following, the thing called akvavit has its own place and deserves its dues.

Stress Reliever

BY RASMUS POULSGAARD

This cocktail was an immediate bestseller. I guess everybody loves a sour and even though I probably wouldn't invent this cocktail today, it is one of the most successful cocktails with regards to turning otherwise sceptic people on to the wonders of akvavit; a proper gateway drug.

The Stress Reliever was a drink invented in theory using the flavour map later presented in this book, put into a simple sour template and abracadabra: a drink was born.

For one drink

4 cl Aalborg Taffel Akvavit
1 cl Falernum (clove, cinnamon, etc.)
1 cl abricot brandy
1 cl gomme
juice of 1/2 a lemon
Dash of egg white

Dry shake and shake with ice. Double strain into a low-ball glass on the rocks and garnish with two slices of cucumber and caraway seeds.

What is it?

2

akvav

It is very difficult, as with any other spirit, to compare the flavours we associate with akvavit today with what started out as a harsh medicinal tonic concocted in apothecaries. One must remember that akvavit, just like gin, has gone through a turbulent journey from being an inferior spirit produced in back yards and farms for the poor to mend their pains and hardships and make them forget the hard labours of life, to a controlled industrial process that focuses on harvesting the wonderful aromatic qualities of caraway, dill, coriander seeds, Seville oranges etc. made for us to savour and enjoy neat and in cocktails.

In the following we will go into some general terminology surrounding akvavit, followed by a run through of the law and production method.

Understanding akvavit in the world of flavoured spirits

In gin, you have different layers in the gin hierarchy as far as production goes, which try to differentiate compound gin from distilled gin and again from London Gin. Those discriminations are a reminiscent of old times when compound gins where flavoured with all sorts of things to mask the rather horrible spirit produced in England and the Scottish lowland at the time, which in turn served as a quality guide so people could avoid subjecting themselves to the worst of sorts. This hierarchy is maybe not as relevant today, as there are wonderful ways of producing compound gins with extractions that complement the juniper distillate and fully live up to the criteria of the highest quality standards.

For the sake of simplicity, you could say that akvavit is a compound spirit, flavoured with distillates of dill or caraway instead of juniper berries, as it in many cases contains extracts to balance and expand the botanical characteristics

> "You could say that akvavit is more of a winter thing in Norway and Denmark being drunk at the Christmas lunches and in some areas for Easter as well, whereas in Sweden the big akvavit occasion is the midsummer parties and the late summer shellfish celebration called 'kräftskiva'."

of the respective akvavit. Adding extracts, or infusions if you will, should therefore not be seen as a mark of inferiority, as it used to be in the gin category, but as a way of adding to the wonderful flavour complexity that is akvavit.

Akvavit, akevitt or aquavit?

Aqua Vitae is, as we have argued, a generic term for spirit adopted by most European languages. In Scandinavia, the shortening *aquavit* sees the light of day in the mid-1500s and slowly the word is integrated into the evolving Scandinavian languages, as exemplified above. We are basically back to the whiskey/whisky discussion with the weird detail that we tend to use *aquavit* when we write in English. We write *akvavit* in this book, because that is how we spell it in Danish.

But akvavit is not just akvavit as the production over time has spread over many countries and continents following the migration of the Scandinavian people, producing many different varieties of the Scandinavian spirit customized for the likings of the native population. In general, you could say that Danish akvavit has a clearer caraway or dill profile, whereas akvavit from Norway carry more anise in the flavour and tend to be cask matured. (These days, the production in Norway is heavily influenced by whisky production, which is quite evident in the profile of most Norwegian cask aged akvavits being released in contemporary times). The akvavits from Sweden are more mildly flavoured with subtle flavours of fennel, caraway and dill compared to their other Scandinavian counterparts. It is a perfect match for shellfish and seafood consumed at their notorious midsummer parties. You could say that akvavit is more of a winter thing in Norway and Denmark being drunk at the Christmas lunches and in some areas for Easter as well, whereas in Sweden the big akvavit occasion is the midsummer parties and the late summer shellfish celebration called "kräftskiva". Maybe that is the explanation for the flavour profile. Who knows.

Taffel

You will find the word "taffel" written on a lot of bottles of akvavit. A taffel akvavit is not a legal definition, but a tradition. Taffel akvavits are white spirits flavoured dominantly, if not exclusively, with caraway. Taffel means "table" in the wider symbolic sense of the table as a place for meeting and dining and rejoicing in the pleasures of food and drink.

The law

Akvavit is produced in many ways depending on the scale of the production and, as mentioned, the place of origin. There is however a set of rules that govern the production and sets boundaries for the category as such. This is not only to dampen the creativity of the producers but also to distinguish akvavit from other spirits and to make sure that it makes sense to talk about akvavit as an entity within the world of spirit.

The legalities behind the akvavit category were forged in 1989 by influential representatives of the akvavit producers of the time under commission by the EU to be able to distinguish akvavit as a category compared to other grain based flavoured spirits such as gin and bitters. The European Union have always been very fond of putting things into boxes, so a box was devised for akvavit as well. Here is an excerpt of the most important implications of the law surrounding akvavit:

→ It must be produced from agricultural ethanol. Which means it cannot be synthesized.
→ It must be at a minimum of 37,5% ABV.
→ Bitter flavours must not affect the taste in a defining manner.
→ Dry matter such as sugar must not exceed 15g per litre.
→ The defining flavours must come from a distillate of either caraway or dill.

Looking at the law the rules come off as quite akin to the restrictions in the gin category. That is because akvavit is, as explained in the previous chapter, similar to gin in many ways both historically and production wise but instead of juniper, an akvavit should be caraway or dill driven.

The first two commandments are quite generic and pretty much common for all spirit types. The third one is there to separate it from the rather big bitter category in Scandinavia and the fourth is obviously there to make sure that there is a border between akvavit and the sweeter liquors.

The most interesting point is really the fifth one, which states that akvavit must be primarily flavoured with distillates of caraway or dill much in the same way as gin has to be primarily flavoured with juniper berries. You could technically make a gin without distilling the botanicals, but this is not the case with akvavit. This means you cannot make akvavit at home, unless you have a still at your house, and you don't. The rule was set up to avoid inferior products tainting the category but the side effect is that akvavit is for professionals only.

Norsk Fatmodnet

Norway has created its own set of regulations called "Norsk fatmodnet" which means "Norwegian cask matured" that can be seen as an addition to the EU legislation. The Norwegian akvavit carrying this label therefore adheres to the EU regulatory system, but also to a set of rules constructed to define the Norwegian part of the category that was not accommodated during the legislative process in EU, since Norway was, and still isn't, a part of the union. The "Norsk fatmodnet" category stipulates that the akvavit must be:

Based on a spirit produced from potatoes and at least 95% Norwegian potatoes. This does not really affect the flavour of the akvavit, as the modern rectifiers produce neutral spirits of such a cleanliness that the base of it is almost undetectable; certainly when mixed with other distillates and extracts. But as with many other things in the world of spirits traditions are important and Norwegian akvavit has almost exclusively been produced from potatoes ever since the Norwegian government in the late 1700s and throughout the 1800s created a widespread potato growing program to boost the economy and to create self-sustainability. This was important at the time because the Napoleonic wars were ravishing Europe and the British navy were blocking the North sea, making it difficult to obtain Danish grain. The potato was perfect for Norway and perfect for producing alcohol, and so the love affair began.

Futhermore it must be cask matured. The size of the barrels determines how long an akvavit must be aged before it can carry the "Norsk fatmodnet" label. If the barrel is over 1000L it has to be aged for over 12 months, if the barrel is under 1000L it only has to mature for over 6 months.

How is akvavit produced?

As explained, akvavit is a basically neutral rectified spirit flavoured with distillates and sometimes extractions. In some instances, it is cask matured before bottling. We will explain the different stages briefly.

Rectification

There is probably no single invention that defines the flavour of akvavit today more than the continuous distillation method, or the process of rectification. It heralded a new era in akvavit production making it possible to produce spirits without the unwanted congeners, such as fusel oil and other by-products which were dominating the flavour of akvavit at the time. Suddenly, it was possible to produce a clean and rectified spirit that did not taint and pollute the botanical mix and desired flavour profile. There is no way of over estimating the influence of this technology in akvavit production and in this way the column still solved a huge array of problems regarding volume of production and purity of outcome.

The rectified spirit is the canvas on which you paint with distillates and extracts to create the flavour profile you want. Its job is to provide a subtle and stabile back drop for the akvavit.

Caraway and Chocolate

BY SUNE URTH

At some point I just stopped writing akvavit in the menu altogether. You can get people to drink anything if you smile and make them relax first. Writing akvavit in the menu in a restaurant was not the way to do that. This one was simply called Caraway and Chocolate, as I was so over finding names for cocktails. Sometimes they had a life span of two weeks before I found something new, and with a minimal list it was just easier to not name them. But it got a life of its own, this one. People started asking for it and ordering it for their friends.

It isn't really a way I would make a cocktail today, it's a bit too straight forward, but the mix of chocolate and caraway is based in pure chemistry. The carvone in caraway is formed during the hydroxylation of limonene and the same two compounds are found in rich amounts in cocoa beans.

For one drink

4 cl Copenhagen Distillery Black Taffel
2 cl Mozart Black or other heavy chocolate liqueur
3 cl lemon juice
1,5 cl simple syrup
One dash tabasco
White of an egg

Dry shake, then shake, and double strain into wine glass. Add a splash of soda. It looks like a beer. Tastes like something very different.

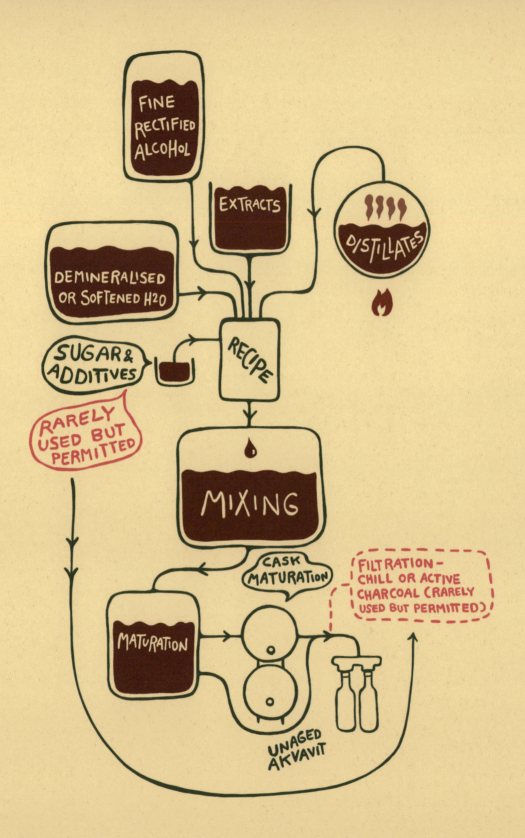

However, it would be wrong to say that the rectified spirit is insignificant. Just because you cannot taste it, it is there, and just as with a house, it is rare to see people compliment the concrete foundation, but when it fails you will notice.

Many producers buy food grade rectified spirits and others distil it themselves. This is not necessarily important as long as you get the quality you want.

A column still works in a drastically different way from a pot still. The column is filled with stacked perforated plates that divide the inside into chambers. The mash with its low alcohol content is fed into the column near the top, and flows down through the holes in the plates.

The still is heated from the bottom, most often by pumping water vapour into it, and as the mash encounters the steam it is vaporised and alcohol and volatiles are forced upwards, while water and solids fall downwards. Every time the rising vapour hits a plate it is condensed, and heavier components are left behind. In this way, the column will purify the mash into a clean distillate, and the distiller can adjust the cleanliness of the product.

This means a column can be fed continuously for days on end and produce a steady stream of clean high quality spirit. It also means that the high-quality spirit will not have the heavy notes of a pot stilled spirit.

Botanical Distillates

We distinguish two methods of flavouring spirit; extraction and distillation. When we talk about distilled flavoured spirits it is important to understand that they are most often made by flavouring a rectified spirit with a distillate of botanicals made in a pot still. A pot still is the basic form of a still. For the purpose of distilling botanicals, a pot is filled with botanicals and rectified spirit, the pot is heated and the alcohol starts evaporating. The heat extracts the aromatic compounds of the botanical into the alcohol (we'll get back to this later under "extraction") and as alcohol boils at a lower temperature than water and the saturation of aromatic compounds change the density of the vapour, we can use the kettle as a sorting hat that separates the liquids.

Through a chilled spiral the vapour is then condensed into a liquid again and collected. The pot still is, as opposed to the column still, very good at retaining aromatic and textural properties in the liquid, which makes it ideal for depositing flavour in a stable manner. The heat separation, or "sorting" of flavour molecules during distillation, also changes the flavour profile wherefore a distillate can taste substantially different from the extraction upon which it is based. This is why it can be interesting to work with distillation alongside extraction when building a flavour profile, something we will elaborate more on in the "mixing" section later.

Extraction, maceration or infusion.

In Scandinavia, the maceration method lives in outhouses and kitchens while the distillation method is, as mentioned earlier, reserved for professionals, as it is blindingly illegal to do at home. Botanicals added to spirit and left on a kitchen shelf is called different things around Scandinavia. In Denmark, we use the word "snaps", the swedes call it "kryddabrännvin" and the Norwegian term is "dram".

An extraction is the same as an infusion or a maceration. When we talk about akvavit, the extracting liquid is either water or rectified alcohol and most often a combination of the two. For the sake of simplicity, we will henceforth use the term extraction. The quality and properties of an extraction are primarily defined by these factors:

→ Temperature
→ Time
→ Strength of the alcoholic solution

At higher temperatures, the solution extracts flavour faster but as some extraction subjects are quite temperature sensitive and lose their desired flavour characteristics at a certain temperature and sometimes produce unwanted ones, one must be careful not to destroy flavours during this process. Most extractions for production of akvavit happens at room temperature.

One would think that the longer the subjects is exposed to the alcoholic solution, the more flavour is extracted, right? This is partly right, but not quite. At one point in the extraction process, an equilibrium is reached in the density of flavour between the extraction subject and the alcoholic solution surrounding it, at which point no more flavour will be extracted. It is also important to note that certain extraction subject over time will develop off flavours, such as bitterness, but also moldy forest, moss, and decay. Ethanol is a solvent and attacks the plant material, so one has to make a conscious choice when it comes to extraction time.

The strength of the extracting liquid largely determine what flavour molecules are extracted in the solution. It has to do with the polarity of the flavour molecule in question.

The arrangement or geometry of the atoms in some molecules is such that one end of the molecule has a positive electrical charge and the other end has a negative charge. If this is the case, the molecule is called a polar molecule, meaning that it has electrical poles. Otherwise, it is called a non-polar molecule.

Whether molecules in an extraction subject are polar or non-polar determine if they will extract in the extraction liquid or not. Also, polar molecules are water soluble, while

> "A practical example: Stawberries in tequila will make a bright red spirit with a light note of strawberries, while strawberries in a water based sugar syrup will make a light pink syrup that tastes like fresh strawberries."

non-polar molecules are soluble in alcohol. What it means from a practical point is that some flavour molecules extract well in alcohol and others extract well in water. Concordantly, when you make an extraction at different alcoholic strengths, you will extract different flavours.

If you, for instance, make an orange infusion at 35% alcohol, you will get a different result than if you were to do the same in a 65% alcoholic solution. This is important to know when you design a flavour profile for an akvavit, as you want to get the exact flavour profile out of a certain subject according to your vision for the end product. But you can also use this when you make infusions for your own bar, at work or at home. Generally speaking, and this is a very general rule of thumb, bitter and dark notes are non-polar, while light, fragrant and flowery notes are polar.

A practical example: Stawberries in tequila will make a bright red spirit with a light note of strawberries, while strawberries in a water based sugar syrup will make a light pink syrup that tastes like fresh strawberries. The flavour molecules are polar and water soluble, while the colour is non-polar and will dissolve better in alcohol.

Mixing

The process of mixing starts at the drawing board, when the product is being planned and designed. There is rarely anything left to chance, as extractions and distillations are expensive to make, but once everything is ready the actual mixing can take place.

Akvavit is compiled of distillations and sometimes extractions to create a harmony. Distillates and extractions can add different dimensions of a flavouring agent, and so extractions and distillations of the same subject can, in combination, make the brain oscillate between the two, and create a more layered and heterogeneous flavour expression.

Sometimes a dash of sugar is added to enhance texture and flavour, but it is rarely used as an actual sweetening agent as there are limits to how much sugar you can add to an akvavit. When we stop looking at these additions as "cheating" and start observing them as active parts of the final product, we begin to understand the art of akvavit mixing.

To sum up, the akvavit mixer takes the rectified alcohol and adds refined distillates and sometimes extractions to create the desired flavour profile. In the process he also adds water to get the right alcohol degree and sometimes a touch of sugar to enhanced and build the flavours. The akvavit is laid to rest for a couple of weeks, or sometimes a bit more to marry the flavours before it is ready for the next step in the process, which is bottling or cask maturing depending on the style of akvavit produced.

Cask Maturing

We have previously described the difference between Norwegian, Swedish and Danish styles of akvavit and the philosophy when it comes to cask maturing. Some akvavits are cask matured and some aren't. We are not going to dive into how and what wood maturing adds to a spirit, something that has been described in great length in other books.

It is an extremely complex process that we are just beginning to understand, as the chemical and biological chain reactions and flavour creations within the cask goes far beyond the obvious wood extraction often credited in literature.

But what is interesting, though, is the fact that deliberate cask maturing has been a part of akvavit production for at least 200 years. It has, more or less, always been a part of the Norwegian style of producing akvavit, something that very much persists in present day.

Normally cask matured akvavits spend between 4 and 24 months in barrels with a few fantastic exceptions to that rule. "Gilde Non Plus Ultra" is aged for 12 years and is to our knowledge the akvavit that rests the longest on wood barrels of all the commercially available akvavits. There are no rules as to what casks one should use for maturing akvavit, but the biggest producer Arcus primarily uses sherry casks. The flavour molecules released during maturation seem to complement the botanicals of the akvavit fantastically, which is something that inspired us to use ingredients that contained the same flavours (clove, vanilla, cinnamon, madeira, sherry, figs and other dried fruits) for mixing with cask matured akvavits in cocktails.

A lot of the aged akvavits are meant for consumption neat and in Norway a lot of people use akvavit all year round as an avec or a digestive after dinner. This is a recent evolution largely driven by the vision of Norwegian akvavit godfather and certified knight of the Norwegian royal order Halvor Heuch, who has managed to place akvavit in the minds

> "That deliberate cask maturing has been a part of akvavit production for at least 200 years."

of the Norwegian people in its well-deserved spot among other high quality spirits.

Just as with Scottish single malts and sophisticated rums, the subtle nuances which gives akvavits their characteristic flavour profile tend to vanish when mixing excessively, but in the hands of a skilled bartender they can produce wonderfully complex spirit driven cocktails that taste like nothing you've had before.

We hope this has given you an understanding of the workings within an akvavit distillery.

We have described all the phases in the production, including the importance of having a properly rectified alcohol as well as a library of extractions and distillates to blend with. We have elaborated on barrel aging, defined and diversified by the skill and preference of the different producers and the cultural traditions surrounding them.

Now we believe it is time for a drink!

A Martini

BY SUNE URTH

I have a soft spot for martinis. It is very much like bartender zen for me. There is nothing to hide behind; just a spoon, some ice and a minimum of ingredients. So making new and interesting martinis is fun but difficult. You sort of need to add that third ingredient, otherwise you're just making a more or less dry martini. This one came out of a strange project about cocktails for Christmas food for a Danish cocktail blog, but it simply works as a good companion for seafood. The trick in it is a very very VERY reduced krieg style wild fermented beer. The beer is simmered on extremely low heat to avoid caramelizing the very few remaining sugars and out of 1 litre of beer I get 50ml reduction. Because there is no sugar left in it after fermentation it doesn't thicken or become syrupy, it just intensifies in flavour. It tastes almost like fish sauce mixed with soy, it's really weird, and salty. Add it to an atomizer and just coat the inside of the chilled glass with it – that will suffice. Apart from that it is fairly straight forward. For multiple servings, I made a massive batch, diluted it and chilled it in the bar freezer, which sits around -1°C, and kept the Krieg reduction in an atomiser.

Serves 10

15 cl Cocchi Americano
50 cl Copenhagen Distillery Dill Anise akvavit
30 cl water

Mix well and chill, store it in a vessel that's good to pour from.
    Arrange in glasses with a mist of reduced Krieg, and serve with a teaspoonful lumpsucker roe on the side if so inclined. Avoid lemon zest.

Tw

leries

A Tale

Dis

Spirit making is an art, a craft and a vocation. We are fortunate to count among our friends a substantial number of producers. The selection of products here is not meant to be derogatory to those not chosen. We have spoken to two producers representing different ends of the spectrum concerning size and approach to akvavit making.

NORDISK BRÆNDERI AND VI.ER AKVAVIT

In Jutland they use the terms Nordenfjords and Søndenfjords to indicate whether something is north or south of Limfjorden, the fjord that cuts through the north of the peninsula. We went Nordenfjords to visit Anders Bilgram, the owner and master distiller at Nordisk Brænderi (Nordic Distillery) and Frederick Krause, the owner of the brand VI.ER AKVAVIT (we.are akvavit), which is made in Anders' pots. We went here to talk to Frederick mainly about the work with VI.ER DANMARK – his taffel akvavit. The distillery is out in the middle of fields with a view of Jammerbugten (bay of moaning – in English 'Bay of Denmark'). A name it takes after the locals who (many years ago) would lure unlucky seafarers to shipwreck in the violent and treacherous Skagerrak ocean in which the bay lies, by running up and down the sand dunes with lamps, to look like ships anchored in safety. The victims of the sand pirates would scream and moan, and there you go.

Anders sailed around the Arctic in an open boat over 8 summers and somewhere along the way he got the idea to make spirit. You get a lot of weird ideas when you sleep on four tanks of very flammable gasoline, apparently. They crashed and toppled the boat twice, recovered it and went

back for more. This earned him a place in the "Adventurers' Club". He is long and sinewy, with kind eyes and a weathered face full of smiles.

Frederick, who is the other half of the collaboration, is 35 years old and decided after having been in marketing and branding for some years as well as having worked as a dive master, been on a reality show in South Africa and marrying a woman from Mexico that corporate life wasn't for him. We are not surprised. He took out a loan and started calling distillers to find someone who would help him. Now they make various products, besides the rather enormous range that Anders makes himself (akvavit and snaps, a few gins, whiskies and brandies. – He also finds time to make rum for Skotlander and a few other things. It would seem he has a deal for an extra day in the week.)

Frederick's akvavit is made with wild caraway seeds from Inderøy (inner island) on the west coast of Norway and juniper berries from the north of Zealand in Denmark. Its priced as a luxury gin and Frederick, with his marketing background, has built a very different universe around it. So what is up with all the naked people?

"It's all about the natural ... our nature. I wanted to make something that I would like and that hopefully other people would like, without the discussion about whether we drink akvavit or not. Caraway is a funny thing, for instance, the stuff I found is from Inderøy in Norway and it's grown wild. They just plant some, let nature take its course over a couple of years and then they

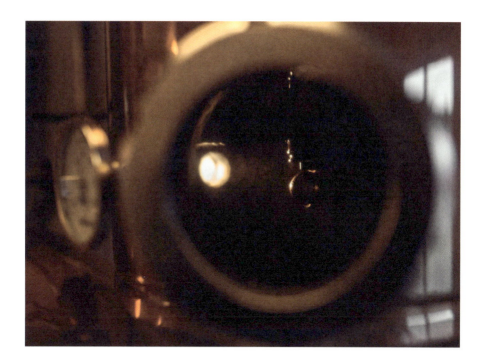

harvest it. I went around Denmark to find botanicals, but as with everything else it wasn't to be that easy.

I had a dream once that I would pick everything by hand, but then I just had to face the fact that there are rules regarding foraging and someone was already doing it a lot better than I ever would be able to.

I ended up sourcing most of our stuff from foragers, who get it directly from our Nordic Mother Nature. I get the juniper berries from the guys who pick herbs for Noma and the caraway from those nutters in Norway".

Anders chips in: "We meet around the kettle here and try out different recipes. I know how the still works, I've worked with it for 8 years, so hopefully I know a bit about what I'm doing. And Frederick has a lot of weird ideas. And between the two of us, we design and create the final spirit."

Nordisk Brænderi has existed since 2009 when Anders got a grant from the local city council. He got the call on a beach in the arctic, because of course you do. For Anders, it's a natural thing to invite co-producers in. Over the years, they've build up a decent production and they are 4 full time employees now. Inviting other people in and nursing their projects is a way to expand the horizon and learn new things – to see new opportunities.

"The idea regarding the juniper", says Frederick, "was basically to tap into the gin market. There is

a huge market for luxury gin and I thought 'why not create a bridge to ease people in their coming transition from gin to akvavit?'

We then quickly realized that the oils from the juniper actually cuts through the ethanol and softens the blow of the normally very harsh first meeting with the akvavit."

We are tasting the raw distillate for the next batch of 100 bottles of VI.ER DANMARK and even at 85% abv it's still soft and palatable.

"In that way, it's a fun journey. I didn't know anything about making alcohol when I started the project, I just knew what I thought was missing – something to make the category sexy again, something to sort of … I don't know, undress? The category?"

All the naked people are about getting back to a Denmark that Frederick knew, summer vacations butt naked on a lawn, the Scandinavian free spirit – the connection with nature, the grassy planty nature, but also human nature.

He frequently uses the term "returning to the old craft" and we laugh a bit about it, as "the old craft" was mainly all about making hazardous hooch and masking it with whatever was around. He admits that storytelling and brand building is important and elaborates:

"If the category is to not only become alive, but especially to thrive, we need to make the category sexier and we need to educate the younger generations. We need to make it sexy for them. A term like "the old craft" might be technically weird, but … In the Nordics, we are known for our craftsmanship, our dedication to quality in every aspect is an ingrained part of our Nordic Heritage and that is what I

am really talking about. One of the things that we are often fighting is that being Nordic is a seal of approval everywhere else except for the Nordics. Only after a product has received international approval, by the media or something similar, then the consumer will start trusting your brand. This has always been a part of the Nordic consumer behaviour that has left me wondering. Why do we need other people far away to tell us that we should like a product that is produced 20 kilometres down the road from you?

We have a very nice lunch at the distillery with Anders and Frederick, then say our goodbyes to Anders, throw Frederick in the back of the car with the kids' seat and set out for Copenhagen. In Danish terms this is about as long a road trip as you can take without leaving the country, so we have plenty of time for talking.

On the ferry crossing the strait between Jutland and Zealand we talk about the importance of having a certain cocktail that drives the category, a thing that will come up again and again as we talk to bartenders around the world.

"I dream", says Frederick, "for VI.ER AKVAVIT to invigorate the akvavit category like Hendricks, Bombay and Monkey 47 did for gin. To make something that would get a new generation excited about the category, to reintroduce it to a new generation. But how do you go about doing that? That's the million-dollar question."

When we travelled Norway teaching bartenders about akvavit, we served akvavit and tonic with a slice of cucumber. In a way, it makes more sense than using it in gin, but we always felt like falling halfway into the pit of serving akvavit as a gin, instead of letting it find its own expression. We have naturally been looking for a way to serve it that wasn't just another something and tonic, even though it is a very easy sell. Guests immediately respond positively to it, but we really don't want akvavit to just be an alternative to gin, because in our perspective it is so much more.

Eetu Topo from Finland came up with the concept of the Pickle, a serve of 2 parts akvavit or other spirit with 1 part stretcher, water, juice, wine or other, and a barspoon each of sweetness and vinegar. This framework works well in skilled hands, but we still need something even simpler.

Apple juice keeps coming back. So does fermented juices on roots or vegetables. Something made with fresh juices that can be tweaked and twisted to the bar's level, but is still easy to replicate at home. We are sure something will emerge.

Building a brand from the bottom is hard work and must be driven by passion and ambition. Frederick has both in abundance. VI.ER AKVAVIT produced just over 1300 bottles in 2016 between the caraway, a dill akvavit and a Christmas akvavit. We are sure to see it grow in the years to come.

AALBORG NORDGULD AKVAVIT AND LARS KRAGELUND

Lars Kragelund holds a master in food science and technology and is employed as Technical director for Arcus Denmark who owns Aalborg Akvavit. We met with him to discuss the latter. He had a big influence on the EU legislative process surrounding akvavit and even invented a new method of freeze distilling.

One of the latest additions to the Aalborg Akvavit portfolio is the Aalborg Nordguld Akvavit – a caraway dom-

inated akvavit with clear notes of citrus and pinewood from an amber distillate and a golden colour from a minimum of 4 months of barrel aging in oloroso sherry casks. Lars headed the team that developed it back in 2007.

At the time, Aalborg was owned by Swedish Vin og Sprit. Market analysis showed a need for a premium akvavit and with a keen eye on the Norwegian tradition of barrel aging, paired with a knowledge of Swedish and Danish tradition of clear(er) spirits, the company expertise was assembled in the form of blenders and food scientists. Instead of making a product to meet explicit demands of consumers they started from within the organisation and made the greatest product they could within the framework of Nordic luxury.

"If we are to purify our trade we need to work that way. In a dialogue with likeminded people. To emerge oneself in the creative accumulation of all our knowledge of food and drink, to let something rise from that – that is the damned art, because it IS art. The better trained a piano player is, the more likely she is to create something beautiful, ok? If we are to change, to evolve, to remake ourselves, we need to let the specialists work in peace. But – if we don't want to lose the people, the public, we need to go and ask them sometimes, otherwise everything is going to turn out as double smoked avant-garde bullshit."

Therefore, a more open process was applied in the finishing stages to let the product interact with reality, gather relevant feedback and subsequently tweak the product accordingly.

"We met up frequently and compared new flavour profiles. It was perfect teamwork as I recall it. Everyone was playing along and no one tried to put their specific signature on

the product. Then we got a board of professional tasters to evaluate and assign points to flavours, both our new ones but also competing products. We then let end consumers taste the flavours and assign a simple 1-10-point score – dislike to like. Then through multivariate data analysis we could discern not only what they preferred, but most importantly why."

The pinewood flavours in the akvavit stem from a distillate made from amber soaked in ethanol, then distilled. The idea, Lars recalls, was first set forth by a marketing company sometime back in the late 1980s. Amber is called "the gold of the north". At the time, it was rejected for being too costly, but 20 years later when the millennial Christmas akvavit for the year 2000 was to be made, it re-emerged. They then kept working with it and it ended up in the Aalborg Nordguld Akvavit (literally "Northern Gold") It just goes to show that it rarely matters where ideas originate; it matters who picks them up and what they do with them.

When Lars was first employed at Aalborg it was hammered into the staff that the words "herbs" and "spices" were not to be used. In Danish, we often use the word "droge" for a component in an alcohol. It's a word that comes from the medicinal background of akvavit.

In this way akvavit retains its link with its remedial ancestry, in that little word droge. A droge can be anything and is in no way limited to botanical compounds. Bones, tusks, rocks, algae, even heart of bear or eye of newt, is fair game.

By soaking amber in ethanol, it is possible to dissolve it as it is not a rock despite the beliefs of many. It is a very dense oil of fossilized pine sap, which you can even hear when you knock it on a firm surface. It sounds soft and warm (amber collectors on the beach knock the rocks on their front teeth to hear if it's sand stone or amber). The ethanol releases the ancient notes of long gone pine forests and used in moderation the amber droge adds complexity and warmth to the flavour profile.

The akvavit was aged in oloroso barrels to round it off and add a touch of sweetness. As far as the flavour profile goes, the choice of oloroso casks over fino or bourbon was not a coincidence. It came back to the tasting boards and

extensive aroma analysis. It would seem, as we touched upon in the former chapter, that sherry wood simply compliments this akvavit better than a bourbon cask.

The product ended up being bottled in a lower, rounder bottle, to complement the rounded flavour profile. The product was finalized and sent to market in 2007. Incidentally the same year Vin & Sprit was purchased by Pernod Ricard. Aalborg Nordguld Akvavit now appears in the well-known Aalborg Akvavit bottle, with a label set in gold and black.

Today akvavit is experiencing a wave of success. And with great success comes great opportunities. Of course the category can take many different turns. Should it do like gin and break down the barriers of the category or stay true to its roots and traditions?

Per se, Lars is not opposed to letting it go crazy, it just isn't for him. He is a strong proponent of dogmas and limitations with the clear view that most good art emerges out of necessity of limitation. But at the same time, he truly believes in keeping a "policy of open doors". We are examples of this, sitting in the heart of the Danish operation talking about recipes for multimillion euro products. He will look you in the eyes and slam his hand in the table to drive his points home like nails in ships.

"I have a hope," he says, hand slamming the table, "that through all the work happening now, we will see an understanding of the joys of the table arise. I believe akvavit belongs on that table and I hope people will share that sentiment. Through these almost spiritual experiences, where it isn't the alcohol talking, but simply the joy of life and food, I believe we become better people and maybe that is a little bit of the way to saving the world."

The Nordic Negroni

BY SUNE URTH

I came from Ruby and was left in charge of the bar at a wonderful restaurant by the waterfront in Christianshavn called no.2, because it was the second restaurant by the owner. The first was AOC with all their Michelin stars.

I was given permission to do an all akvavit menu and it went rather avant-garde at times. I bought a small still and started making my own gins and akvavits by reinfusing bottles of vodka with botanicals.

The first cocktail I made for the menu was this one, the Nordic Negroni. It has been on the menu ever since. Everyone likes it. The cocktail ended in a study at University of Copenhagen where we compared different ages on bottle aged Negronis with aroma analysis and sensory blind test by a panel of bartenders. The results were quite interesting. It would appear that after about 3 months the evolution of the aroma profile slows down. This force fused version had most similarity with a product around 9 months old, but it wasn't an exact replica, it was something new. Yay nerds!

Adjust according to number of guests or thirst.

Equal parts of
Campari
Martini Rosso
Aalborg Nordguld

For each set of bottles, add the thin peel of one orange. Divide in vacuum bags, vacuum seal and submerge in 45°C water for 90 minutes. Let cool completely and bottle. Serve on the rocks.

Alternatively combine in bottle and leave for 3-9 months. Serve as above.

Akva

bad

vit

abro

Every place around the world that pay any attention to cocktails have their own story of how they went from producing fast paced drinks with more attention to the colour of the beverage than to what was in it, to becoming a city with trained bartenders with moustaches and waistcoats, who, if they found you worthy, could tell you the mash bills in every bourbon in their back bar and how to use it in a new-found forgotten classic that nobody but themselves cared about.

And so, when the present cocktail revolution hit the Scandinavian countries shortly after Y2K (yes millennials, the struggle was real) Scandinavia too was quick to adopt the culture. We embraced punches, slings, fizzes, old fashioneds, manhattans and the prohibition era, just as almost every other bartender on the planet wanting to rediscover the almost lost craft of proper bartending. We focused on fresh juices and other ingredients, on delivering the best possible products to our guests. This was a very important period and a necessary one at that, but what we did was not specifically Scandinavian nor Danish. Rather we found inspiration in visits to cities like London and New York. When we started this project, it was only natural that we would retrace our steps and revisit the places that had influenced us the most as well as been the driving force of the modern cocktail revolution.

And so, we packed our suitcases and went out to talk to bartenders we knew worked with akvavit. We were curious as to how bartenders from a completely different culture perceived and worked with a spirit, we considered to be ours.

LONDON

SUMMER 2016

London is lovely in its hideous glory. Our hotel room is a cell in a labyrinth, cold dirty walls in the hallway, flickering lights like something out of a horror cliché. The room itself with its balcony overlooks Old Street tube station and happens to be very close to many bars that we feel morally obliged to frequent in the name of science and journalism. We eat decently but without presumption.

After ECC in Chinatown for drinks on akvavit and Chinese food around the corner, we hop on a bus and head out to Original Sin.

Original Sin

Original Sin is a basement dive in the best sense of the word. Located behind an inconspicuous store front and down the stairs, the room unfolds in dark wood and naked bricks.

We sit down to talk to Cyan Wong, who's in charge of affairs this evening.

Original Sin is the sister bar of Happiness Forgets of well-earned fame. Original Sin is an attempt to make a neighbourhood bar and judging by the clientele on a Monday afternoon they are succeeding. There is that distinct local vibration in the air, everyone is, if not old friends, then at least acquainted.

"We both recall the first time we saw an American tourist taste akvavit and light up with the word passionfruit on her lips."

Akvavit came to OS through Happiness Forgets. The selection on the first back bar was very limited and it was natural to search for ingredients that could make it stand out.

The way Happiness Forgets and Original Sin utilize Akvavit is, as we learn over the next days, not unusual. It appears as a spice, as a modifier. In the Penfold Sour we find 15ml of Linie Aquavit and in the Angel Fizz just 7. But notice how it actually stands as a main component in the Penfold Sour as everything else is fortified wine. And in Angel Fizz it appears as a bridge between the different grains.

Cyan is the first to mention a thing that will follow us for the next year in our travels. Bartenders from outside of Scandinavia have a completely different angle on akvavit

than us of Norse decent. Cyan compares the caraway notes to pickled lemon and passionfruit and describes it as a fresh addition to the flavour bouquet. We both recall the first time we saw an American tourist taste akvavit and light up with the word passionfruit on her lips. To us at that time, the comparison was insane, caught as we were in the trauma of being a teenager in Scandinavia.

ANGEL FIZZ

20ml Bourbon Whisky
20ml Rye Whisky
20ml Chinato de Vergano
7ml Linie Aquavit
20ml lemon juice
20ml simple syrup
A dash of egg white

Shaken, then strained into glass.
Boozy yet refreshing, the chinato wine adds depth and longevity. The akvavit leaves little notes of herbs on the long aftertaste.

PENFOLD SOUR

20ml Byrrh Aperitif
20ml Kamm and Sons
   British Aperitif
15ml Linie Aquavit
20ml lime juice
A dash of egg white
10ml sugar cane syrup

Shaken then double strained.
Layered notes of bitterness flows into acidity and warmth. Surprisingly fruity with an elegant caraway finish.

White Lyan

White Lyan were on the World's 50 best list for years, and with good reason. The amount of afterthought and contemplation that went into the cocktail making was astounding and the consistency with which it was executed was, and remains, awe inspiring. We print the rest of the interview as it was written in the days after the visit.

Alistair Kelsey is behind, and in front of, the bar on this Tuesday afternoon. We seem to have a talent for overlooking the entrance; an unmarked door in a white storefront. After a bit of walking back and forth we find it but this isn't the first time here for any of us and it isn't the first time we can't find it either.

The White Lyan approach is well known in the industry now, but when they started out it was an outlandish concept that a lot of people shook their heads at.

Everything is prepared prior to service. There are no fresh juices – the bar does not even have an ice well. Instead freezers and fridges dominate the back bar and from there the bartenders pull forth bottles of coloured liquids, paints, gels and atomizers. And it sounds very much like circus mixology, but there is method to the madness.

The point is to liberate the energy spent in service. Under the assumption that the energy is constant, it was a logical step for owner Ryan C to move said energy from the repetitive task of preparing drinks in front of the guests to being a host and a partaker of peoples' evenings.

This in turn leaves space for weird ingredients and strange concoctions.

As we are talking, a couple of guests walk in and the fact that the interview doesn't really stop is a brilliant example of how efficient the method is. It's just an ongoing conversation that involves whoever walks through the door. Including the hobo guy who wants to sell us 3 pounds of ground meat.

In the Purple Paint the 'akvavit' used is not actually an akvavit for legal reasons. It's a caraway flavoured gin made in the basement. We ask about it.

"Yes, we are fully well aware that it not legally an akvavit, but we needed a very distinct flavour profile and so we created that profile," says Alistair. And this opens an interesting talk about properties in spirits in cocktails. The White Lyan approach is that a Rye Whisky, for instance, needs to be able to give a distinct rye flavour to a cocktail, not necessarily be palatable or delicious in its own right. It gets its necessity only in the mixing. So, the fact that it is not actually an akvavit does not bother them at all. Just like it doesn't bother us since the result is great.

The place is very subtle in its art. Slightly transparent walls reveal traces of underlying mechanics, and gives a feeling of being very close to the actual secret of it all, and yet have it just out of reach. And it's subtle, not even something they use as a focal point, it's just there, behind it all.

White Lyan is artful in its concept, but down to earth in the execution and this is the true art. To have something so conceptual as a bar without ice, and deliver it, as if it was just another pub. To use it to make people relax, instead of intimidating them with "mixology", is inspiring at the very least.

"The place is very subtle in its art. Slightly transparent walls reveal traces of underlying mechanics, and gives a feeling of being very close to the actual secret of it all, and yet have it just out of reach. And it's subtle, not even something they use as a focal point, it's just there, behind it all."

PURPLE PAINT

Make "Akvavit"
Toast In a pan:
2g cardamom
8g pine nuts
10g caraway
1.5g cinnamon bark
0.5g star anise
2g pink peppercorns

Add to 500ml of mr lyan vodka & sous vide for 2 hours at 60ºC
Strain solids off and blend with mr lyan gin. 1500ml gin to 500ml spiced vodka (3:1)

Make Aronia syrup
800g sugar
60g citric acid powder
20g ground dried aronia berries
120g Lemon distillate
2000g Boiling water

Whisk all ingredients until the powders are dissolved. Strain through superbag once cooled.

Vat drink
3000g aquavit
2500g water
3000g aronia syrup
50g Blueberry distillate (Can use blueberry juice, syrup or blueberry instead!)

Serve: Blackcurrant paint on prohibition glass, 85g batch, lemon distillate over the top.

Boozy like a Manhattan, with sweetness and acidity from the berries. A fresh minty feel from the very forward caraway. Almost dry, tart aftertaste, mouth drying turns into salivating. The creamy paint cheats the mouth into expecting a jammy cocktail, yet the high alcohol challenges that, leaving thoughts of summer fruits soaked in booze.

Callooh Callay

Callooh Callay is one of those places you always come back to. It did not help us on this trip that we lived around the corner and they are open until late every day. We spoke to Bobby Hiddleston, who is no longer there, about new flavours and how to sell them.

When working with akvavit, Bobby told us, they first tried using templates from other cocktails, gin cocktails mainly. And it worked well. But they felt a need to move beyond that and use the complex deep spices on their own accord.

Bobby talks about cocktails driving categories. Gin has the gin and tonic and the dry martini, whisky has a whisky neat and whisky sour and rum has the Cuba Libre and the Daiquiri. Tequila even has a few, but akvavit has … well, nothing. "So", Bobby said, "when the end user is standing in a supermarket with a bottle of akvavit they don't know what to do with it".

FISHERMAN'S RIVAL

40ml Linie Aquavit
20ml Dolin Blanc
20ml lemon juice
15ml sugar syrup
20ml egg white
2 dashes of celery bitters
A pinch of salt
A pinch of pepper

Light and refreshing. Clear caraway notes with a touch of anise. The sweetness from the Dolin is underlined by the pepper and celery.

In Scandinavia, we drink it neat with food, but introduce that concept to non-Scandinavians and they look at you like you have two heads. The basic idea of drinking hard alcohol as a food pairing seems to border on sacrilege, apparently. According to Bobby, if we want to secure akvavit a place on the shelves in the future, we need to talk about ways to consume it that transcends tradition.

MOUNTAIN SPRING

20ml Vodka
10ml pine needle akvavit
40ml Saké
10ml jasmin syrup
40ml soda
Rocks glass full of ice
Garnish with a long slice of cucumber

Serving like a vodka and soda, this little number packs a secret or two. The akvavit is infused with fresh pine needles that play catch with the jasmine notes. The Saké adds depth and dryness.

NEW YORK

FALL 2016

We've both been here many times and love coming back. We're staying in Williamsburg this time around. We have a first floor of a townhouse owned by a young couple. We eat everything fast. Tacos on lower Manhattan, pizza and wonderful, strong anduja at Roberta's. Massive amounts of mac'n cheese and bbq at some place we never got the name of and pastrami sandwich to die for at Harry and Ida´s deli. Lobster rolls Maine style, burgers at Burger Shack to finish off in the airport. And cocktails, cocktails, cocktails. But we are here for a reason.

Nomad

The Nomad Hotel opened in 2012. With its bombastic elephants it quickly became a New York Hotspot with guests queuing through the restaurant to get in. Not wanting to make people wait, or upset the dining guests, the group (who also runs 11th Madison) purchased an adjacent house and opened a new bar.

Leo, who's been with the group for 11 years, built the cocktail program around his love for the classics. New York is fortunate enough, he says, to actually have seasons, which means that things go in and out of availability as the year progresses. This means that their cocktail list, at any given time numbering 50-60 different cocktails,

change. Every 3 months 8-10 cocktails will go out and a new set is put in. Some cocktails stay on the list for years, others only get a few months to shine.

Akvavit came to the bar by complete accident. When Leo took over 11 years ago, there was a massive stock of left over spirit from the old bar menu. Tons of sherry and a huge pile of OP Anderson Akvavit. He started playing around with it and one night ended up at the late Vandaag, where Katie Stipe (Flatiron Lounge, Bourgois Pig, Grand Army) had done an all Akvavit cocktail menu, which sold him on the concept.

When asked about the future for akvavit, Leo has no doubt that the cocktail approach is fruitful. Americans drink wine and beer with food. He does not see the Scandinavian tradition of having akvavit as food companion as something that will get big in the states. However, the American drinking public is adventurous and always ready for new flavours and akvavit as a cocktail component is quickly earning its place in the back bar.

CAFÉ CON LECHE

- 1/2 ounce cold brew coffee
- 1/2 ounce Rhum Clement Creole Shrubb
- 3/4 ounce orgeat
- 3/4 ounce lemon juice
- 1 ounce Eldorado 12yo
- 1 ounce Linie Aquavit
- Float of coffee infused angostura bitters

Shake and double strain into coupette.

The Café con Leche is inspired by the Italian anise cakes from Stella D'oro that Leo would have with coffee when he was a teenager at his grandmother's.

"The American drinking public is adventurous and always ready for new flavours"

NORTH SEA OIL

1/4 ounce Combier triple sec
1/2 ounce Laphroaig 12yo
3/4 ounce Cocchi Americano
1 1/2 ounce Linie Aquavit

As a kid, Leo would eat orange/fennel candy, a sweet whose name eludes him but the flavour lingered. He first tasted Linie Aquavit in the mid naughties and immediately picked up on the anise and wanted to turn it into a cocktail reminiscent of his childhood sweet. The cocktail was meant as a snide joke and ended up being a house favourite, still seeing orders even though it's been off menu for half a year.

Mace

Mace is the brain child of Nicolas de Soto, former head bartender at ECC in London and New York. We both met him in our days at Ruby and since then kept running into him through guest shifts in Copenhagen, New York and London – one of them during the Ruby appearance at Manhattan Cocktail Classics. After several years at ECC, he wanted to make his own place and after not finding a suitable venue in London he came back to New York.

The narrow space on 9th street is laid out as a modern spice shop with rows of herbs and spices in jars on the shelves. The cocktails, 12 in the menu, are named solely after their main spice and thus cocktails like Yerba Mate and Long Pepper grace the pages along with botanical drawings of plants and seeds. The ingredients are fairly complicated at times, but as all the prepping is done before guests arrive the expression of the bar is one of cool energy surplus and wide eyed wonder.

Nico ran across akvavit back in 2010 working in London. He starts talking, still slightly windy from the trip here and the fact that he arrived straight from work-out. He speaks softly, with a distinct French tone to his English, his voice an almost timid contrast to his tall slender frame.

"I would use it to spice up a vodka drink because I hate vodka drinks – they are very boring – and then I used more and more akvavit and less and less vodka, and voila, here we are."

Nicolas has an impressive collection of the stuff. We count 12 different examples of akvavit, which is shocking for a bar in the states.

"I do not," he says with his heavy French British, still uncoloured by his years in New York, "I do not imagine akvavit being everywhere anytime soon. It will be here, but quiet, yeah? Here, the Americans they do not drink it with the food, but again, they do not drink it when they are teenagers, they think of it as exotic, yeah?"

VALHALLA RISING

3/4 ounce lime juice
3/4 ounce ginger syrup
1 ounce Linie Aquavit
1 ounce oloroso sherry

Shake and strain into highball full of ice, garnish with dried ginger on a stick.

The fact that akvavit is introduced quite late to experienced drinkers, instead of to teenagers who just drink to get smashed, means that the flavours can stand as individual spices, instead of being this dreaded nightmare that a lot of Scandinavians connect them with. So, the Easter or Christmas excess stigma that akvavit still is connected to in Scandinavia does not exist, rather it's seen as an exotic and interesting flavour.

MACE

3/4 ounce coconut syrup from young coconut milk
1/2 ounce beetroot juice balanced with orange acid
1 ounce Aperol
1 ounce Linie Aquavit
Extract of mace sprayed on top

Shake and strain into coupette, spray mace tincture on top.

Up&Up

Chaim Dauermann is a smallish chap with a bushy moustache and quick fidgeting fingers. He talks fast, moves fast, then stops mid-sentence to contemplate the wording of a potential utterance. We walked to the basement where Up&Up resides through a very jazzy neighbourhood. Had iced cold brew coffee on the corner and walked down the stairs.

    The basement bar is dark even in the clear late summer light. Chaim is cleaning vigorously to make everything very shiny for the photos. He stops the camera when he spots a fleck of dust on a table, corrects invisible details. His hands are fluttering like insane butterflies and then freeze mid-air, only to flutter on moments later. We talk lengthily about all the things that Chaim is passionate about.

"I definitely see a future for akvavit, yes, definitely, it's a great thing, it has a place here. You know, bartenders know it, we had a guest come in, he was from Sweden, he looked at the menu, he said 'why do you use akvavit, you're insane!' and we don't think we are, it tastes really good, we got the Brennivin (akvavit from Iceland) after a trip to Iceland, we fell for it completely, we had to use it, you know."

He talks like that, for 45 minutes, small breaks to correct a coaster that seem to have snuck into the frame, then back to the sentence.

"Education, really, bartenders know what's going on, but it's a long way to the … the … end consumer, you know, but how to reach them? The bars can only do so much right? But availability maybe. We can get Linie Aquavit over here, maybe OP (Anderson) if we're lucky. Krogstad and Gamle Ode, but they are American… "

There are a lot of American distilleries now making akvavit. There are the dedicated producers, like Gamle Ode and Old Ballard who only produce akvavit and then there are a bunch of distillers who make an akvavit or two on the side of their whisky and gin productions, like Bullrun and Long Road Destillers just to mention a couple. In a few years, as demand

ROSE AMONGST THORNS

2 dash Gary Regans orange bitters
1 ounce Krogstad Akvavit
1 ounce Citadel Gin
1/2 ounce Amaro di Montenegro
1/2 ounce Dolin dry
Stir and serve up with a lemon twist

A golden and flavourful Manhattan/Martini-ish thing, the Rose Amongst Thorns combines the anis profile from Krogstad with sweet bitterness from Amaro di Montenegro using the lightness of the gin as a bridge between the two.

> "We've already talked about the regional differences within Scandinavia, but the American approach is a new leg on the pot. From our experience, they seem more anise driven with a more discreet botanical expression than their Scandinavian counterparts."

rise and the distribution channels are set up properly, we'll hopefully see a lot more Scandinavian akvavits in the states. The demand is there, not solely, but in large part due to the fact that a very significant number of millions of Americans consider themselves Scandinavian by descent.

There is a difference between Scandinavian and American akvavit. We've already talked about the regional differences within Scandinavia, but the American approach is a new leg on the pot. From our experience, they seem more anise driven with a more discreet botanical expression than their Scandinavian counterparts.

THAT'S WHY

1 ounce Brennivin Akvavit
1 ounce Mezcal
1/2 ounce St Germain
1/4 ounce Ancho Reyes chili liqueur
1/4 ounce red bell pepper syrup (simple syrup blended with red bell pepper, then strained through fine cloth)
Stir and serve on ice w grapefruit twist

A collaboration between Katie Byrum and Chaim. The name came along when a drunk patron decided to not leave and responded to all approaches, even threats of calling the police, with a firm "That's why". The Brennivin from Iceland plays a supporting role while the mescal and the Ancho Reyes builds a powerful wall of aroma. The red bell pepper syrup is, even on its own, very interesting and swirls its way in between the sheets of flavour.

Akvavat

5

it a

home

When we started the journey of discovering akvavit and experiencing the wonderful flavours that the Nordic spirit had to offer, we also immediately started experimenting with substituting the base spirit in classic recipes with akvavit. We quickly found out that gin based cocktails substituted with Danish and Swedish akvavit made sense because of its clean and botanically driven flavour, but also that the Norwegian akvavits, which are primarily cask matured, in some instances could be used as substitution for whisky or even dark rum. It was an epiphany for us to discover the diversity of the spirit and to experience that the new combinations added new Nordic flavours to our beloved classics and in some cases made them even better!

Soon after, we started to experiment with akvavit as a starting point for flavour pairings to uncover the true potential of the spirit in a mixing context. We made cocktails that looked like cocktails out of the Caribbean, American and southern European traditions with Nordic ingredients and found wonderful combinations and drinks.

We wanted to explore in detail how other Scandinavian bartenders had ventured into the world of akvavit. To hear their thoughts on the subject, to compare notes. But we got a lot more than that.

SWEDEN   WINTER 2016/17

Hay Market

Someone once described Stockholm as "the Venice of the North" which is utterly ridiculous. But what is not ridiculous is Stockholm in its own right. The beautiful Swedish capital is built on a number of islands in the ragged country connecting the lake Mälaran with the Baltic Sea. The city is sprawling with bars and restaurants to cater to the needs of the more than 2 million people living in the greater metropolitan area.

One of them is Johan Evers, former bar manager at Corner Club, world class top 10 finalist and – as this book goes into printing – a partner and manager at Penny & Bill.

We find him, however, on a cold November day in 2016 at the Haymarket, a Scandic hotel fitted in fancy 1920's garbs, art deco staircases, monkeys hanging from the walls carrying lightbulbs, crazy and fun times galore. The hotel is from April 2016 with 8 floors of beautiful rooms.

Here he runs a small pop-up in the penthouse suite, taking in three seatings a night of a maximum of 14-15 people at the time, and akvavit is a natural element on the menu.

"It's fun because it's difficult. People say it's a lot like gin, but that's not right, it works completely different. It has a strong edge in the flavour that will not hide, it always reveals its presence. It's very cultural. We have that warning in the back of our head, the nose tells of horrid drinking and bad behaviour. That's what we struggle with: trying to get guests to enjoy it."

Johan compares it to that warning you can get from tequila or grappa, your brain telling you we are dealing with hard alcohol. And that warning has nothing to do with any property of the liquid; it is naught but a triggering of the lizard brain trying to get you to stay away from something that once made you sick.

SOMETHING WITH OLIVES

35 ml Linie Aquavit
25 ml gin (hearty and juniper forward)
20 ml lime juice
5 ml olive brine

Top with homemade soda: Water, lime, fresh mint and Menthe Pastille to taste. Carbonate in chiffon. Garnish with olive branch.

The Scandinavian culture of drinking akvavit has very little to do with moderation. But using it in cocktails, with the behaviour patterns that brings with it, is a way of changing the public perception of the category.

Johan thinks in flavour pairings as he makes new cocktails, but the booze comes last. He used to do it the other way around, booze first, then direction, sweet or sour, stiff or fresh and then a balancing, but woke one morning with a sense of being strangled creatively. And he was eating a Greek salad and thinking about the combination of olives and mint in it and then thinking what spirit would be good with it and it turned into the cocktail "Something with Olives" (page 112).

We talk about the future. About more and more bars using akvavit and the varying results.

"A lot of bartenders overcomplicate it. We need to make it simpler if people are to understand [akvavit in cocktails]. Like Blacktails in New York who reinvented Cuban classics, maybe we should reinvent a few simple cocktails as akvavit cocktails? Why not just make an akvavit Collins, it's nice and easy, it's a good beginning."

And he calls for education – of bartenders and guests alike. We are finding a strong identity in our food culture, but we know nothing about our own spirits. Scandinavia is the cool kid in town on the global food scene, maybe it's time to let the spirit shine?

LIGHT UP AND BEETROOT

40 ml OP Andersen
20 ml homemade yellow beet vodka
20 ml house blend vermouth (blended with a touch of peach and Gammel Dansk Bitter)

Stirred and served up. In-out zest of lemon sprayed from high altitude. Garnish with crisps of beet on the side.

Open/Closed

We touch down in Umeå in snow. Pine forests cover the rocky hills, the river is frozen and the airport is a collection of red wooden shacks. 120.000 people huddle together in Umeå in the north of Sweden. There is a distinct "last stop before nothing"-feel, the cab driver is talkative and offers to pick us up later – "just give me a call" – and the sun sets at 2pm this time of year.

We meet Emil Åreng at Stora Hotellet (literally "the big hotel) for a talk about cynical old men with angry beards and an industry that's gotten lost on Instagram.

After years of working at a classic cocktail joint called Rex, he wanted to open shop on his own but being a bartender and not having any money, he also wanted someone to pay for it. Finally, he found two guys who were opening a deli and they decided to make something they hadn't seen before.

Open/Closed is a small venue in a deli in the courtyard behind Stora Hotellet. Courtyard is misleading. The space behind the hotel is covered in glass, houses a restaurant and the deli, opens up to the city library, a self-service hotel and another restaurant.

At the Open/Closed Emil makes simple no-nonsense drinks. They clear a table in the middle of the deli, put up 24 barstools and make 600 drinks a Week

The menu changes every two weeks and will always consist of a low- or no-alcohol drink, a stiff, a refreshing thing and a dessert. Apart from that there are three seasonal cocktails that change with the weather. The menu theme is up in the air. As we visit it is Star Wars, because December is Star Wars month, apparently. And then Emil lifts the curtain on a very different way of making drinks.

"I don't really do flavour that much, that's Karl-Martin, my partner in crime, I am just really good at lying", he starts out saying. The duality is rather profound: on one hand he seems hell bent on cutting away bullshit and getting to the actual point, on the other hand he openly admits that sometimes they lie and make up stuff to make ends meet in their cocktails. And if you are honest about lying, is it then such a bad thing?

"We start with the story", he then says, much to our amusement, "and then build the flavours around that. Like a thing we did mashing up "Imagine" by John lemon and Nas' "Illmatic" which has nothing to do with each other, but yeah, we got

the cognac from Nas, but not Hennessy, that's nasty, and then changed John's last name to lemon because the only fruit he sings about is a strawberry and Nas is a fucking poet so he doesn't need fruit, and you know, then Yoko Ono sort of destroyed John's life and Yoko means sparkle in Japanese, so we destroy the drink with sparkling water and it's still a good drink but would have been better without the bubbles and … it sounds really pretentious saying it out loud, but it's a really fun way to work. It's hard, right? Going just by flavour is too easy. We don't like easy."

One of the readings of the Japanese signs for Yoko could be sparkling child, but it's in the meaning of light sparkling. But it just serves as an example of the mythomanic honesty that surrounds the project. Catch him lying and it's part of the show.

Anyway, the story is created first with a base in the theme, then the cocktail must evolve from that. There are rarely any garnishes as Emil, in his own words, is unable to cut anything nice from a lemon. The snide sarcasm covers something much deeper though. A thorough river of conviction running through his words when he speaks.

SCANDILICIOUS

50 ml OP Anderson Aquavit
20 ml spruce syrup
150 ml warm coffee

Build in toddy glass. Float cream flavoured with cloudberry syrup
To make the spruce syrup, take one litre of simple syrup and add a branch of Norwegian spruce. Leave it for 24 hours. Filter.

For the cloudberry cream, add 200g cloudberries to a litre of warm simple syrup. Leave for 5 hours and strain. Then mix one part cloudberry syrup with two parts cream.
In a suitable glass, add akvavit and syrup and mix. Pour in the warm coffee and close with cloudberry cream.

"We got so caught up in Instagram and Facebook, we forgot where we came from. Why do you care what someone likes on Instagram? We're so busy dressing things up nicely and taking pictures and posting and reading magazines about what is trending and I hate that word, it's obnoxious, that we forget what the guest in front of us want, you know? What do I care what some idiot in Sidney or Singapore thinks is trendy? They have different stuff, it doesn't matter to me!"

Forgetting where we come from, it's a reoccurring topic in Emil's stream-of-consciousness talking. We should talk to our elders, go chat with our grandparents and reinvent the flavours and smells of our childhoods.

"We can't make Indian cuisine, it's not in our DNA, I mean, I love it, and I try making it, but I have no idea what it is supposed to taste like. I can follow a recipe, but it's not in my blood. But the birch woods around here, the explosion of a cloud berry in my mouth in summer and the smell of moss, that's my blood, that's my DNA."

It's the whole going away to get inspired thing that gets on his nerves. He wants us to go backwards in time instead, go inward, reinvent ourselves. And akvavit is a natural step as a bartender in Scandinavia. He sees the fading of the borders between chefs and bartenders as a means for salvation here. All the flavours in the Nordic kitchen flow into the Nordic spirit, and we can utilize those in cocktails.

Akvavit, to Emil, is something quite special. The herbaceous notes are more complex and rich than the profile of a gin, and the sharp notes of dill and caraway is something very different from the vanilla and toffee of a whisky. He starts making an old fashioned on Linie Aquavit. Tells a story about how Umeå burned to the ground in 1888 and was rebuilt using only birch. And the birch syrup he uses for sweetening is made simply by reducing birch water using very low heat, from 100 to 1 litre. The price tag is astronomic but the taste is rich and sweet and the flavour enhancing properties in birch water is enhanced. He adds a dash of salt and a healthy measure of Linie Aquavit onto a massive chunk of ice from a bit north of here that is either hand harvested and trucked in for the express purpose of this very drink, or just something he had lying around, depending on what mood he is in.

The first time Emil tried incorporating akvavit in a cocktail was his entry for world class 2010. He messed around a bit with the vodka that was supposed to be used

"One of the readings of the Japanese signs for Yoko could be sparkling child, but it's in the meaning of light sparkling. But it just serves as an example of the mythomanic honesty that surrounds the project. Catch him lying and it's part of the show."

and ended up adding akvavit, butter, salt and dill. He was sold instantly and akvavit has been a part of his stable ever since.

For Emil it all boils down to connecting with your heritage, with the soil beneath your feet. The future has to anchor itself in the past. We need to look past trends and what looks nice in a post everyone forgets immediately. Emil dreams of a bar that uses only Nordic ingredients, without shortcuts. A massive movement for Nordic spirits, the abandonment of lemons and basil. Emil swears and dreams and shakes his long black beard. And in his foraged weird little bar his guests can forget about Instagram and reposts for one night at the time.

BOLD FASHIONED

60 ml Linie Aquavit
15 ml Birch Syrup
2 dash Angostura Bitters

Add all ingredients to rocks glass with large ice cube. Stir until properly diluted.

Familjen

We fly in over Göteborg, or Gothenburg as it is known in English. The lights are little pebbles in the darkness and in the distance, across the water, the northernmost tip of the Danish peninsula of Jylland (Jutland) would be visible if not for the clouds and the fact that it's pitch black night.

Just over half a million people live their lives here. It's the fifth largest city in Scandinavia and a great place for beer and cocktails. Without this turning into a tourist guide, they have an excel-

> "I like to go out of town, I have a small place out in the woods, I like to go out there and kill the sound on my phone and take a long walk and pick stuff. It's great, I recharge, it's my comfort zone."

lent opera, beautiful scenery by the water and very friendly people. It reminds us a bit of Copenhagen, with the canals and the old houses. Just a bit smaller.

The summer in Göteborg starts with "Colours", an annual hip-hop festival/club hosting concerts and events since 2007. Tom Surma makes a little bar called Tom's cocktailbar and every week, as the festival's colour theme changes, so does the colour of the weekly akvavit based cocktail. This playfulness, fun cocktails in fun colours, appears to be symptomatic for his work.

Tom is an ambassador for the Swedish akvavit OP Anderson and the manager at renowned Familjen (the Family), a bar and restaurant in downtown Göteborg with a laidback bistro kitchen and a seasonally influenced cocktail bar.

"I like to go out of town, I have a small place out in the woods, I like to go out there and kill the sound on my phone and take a long walk and pick stuff. It's great, I recharge, it's my comfort zone."

We talk a lot about comfort zones. Tom's cap says "dedicated", on the back bar another cap sports a "hip-hop and cocktails", there's a small basketball hoop and lots of wrinkled photos tagged to the walls and boxes. Tom has been running it since 2009, when he was offered the job by the restaurant, who realized they needed a cocktail bar due to popular demand. He dragged his partner in crime Victor Peterson with him from the cocktail bar "Lokal" which unfortunately no longer exists and today it's a tight four-man operation with very good reviews.

"If you can get your guests into your comfort zone, they relax, you can take them everywhere… Make it fun, selling is about having fun, if we don't have any guests, we don't have any jobs. Make people, I don't know, lead them? Make it interesting, if it's too hard, if they don't get it, they'll go to their own comfort zone."

But if we can get them to accept our comfort zone as their own, we can take them for a ride, is the essence of his philosophy. Tom also trains other bars for OP Anderson and the comfort zone concept is a part of this as well. To make akvavit part of a bartending comfort zone, to make it the bottle you grab for when someone asks for something fun, instead of having it sitting in the back bar as an intimidating monolith.

SHORT & BOOZY

50 ml OP Anderson Aquavit
10 ml Gammel Dansk Bitter
1 bspn simple syrup
20 ml pilsner beer
3 dashes Angostura Bitter
1 pinch sea salt

Served on block ice with a side of pickled rowanberries. It looks like a cloudy old fashioned. The beer adds a touch of acidity and the Gammel Dansk (a Danish stomach bitter quite heavy on pepper and cinnamon) makes it sweet and wintery. OP Anderson is a lighter, but typically Swedish, akvavit that puts a flowery fennel quite forward in the picture.

"Start with something easy, don't make it too hard for yourself or your guests, they get scared. Just make an akvavit and tonic, it doesn't have to be dancing monkeys and crazy infusions, it can just be simple."

There is a very clear image in Tom's head when we talk about the universe surrounding akvavit. It comes out in cut up bursts of words, interspersed with pauses, as he searches for the precise words to make the image come alive. It's not the wild flavours of the Tiki or the dark smell of dusty books from the gentlemen's parlour. It's an image of wild rivers and clean air. Simple architecture and light. Snow on boots and fire, birch wood and sorrel and crisp apples and honey. The Scandinavian minimalism as flavour.

In his work as ambassador Tom has a chance to help shaping the new generations of bartenders. It's about education, even though he hates the word. The philosophy cuts through again. To allow bartenders to adopt akvavit as a natural part of their vocabulary, to help create a universe, a frame of reference, it's something that makes the little hairs on Tom's arms stand up like soldiers.

APPLES AND FENNEL

50 ml apple infused OP Anderson Aquavit
10 ml Yellow Chartreuse
30 ml apple juice from the south of Skåne
30 ml lemon juice
20 ml fennel syrup

Shaken and served in a Collins glass on the rocks. Served with a side of deep fried sourdough flavoured with fennel and fresh apple.

NORWAY

WINTER 2016/17

Raus

Raus on the Corner of Nordra and Carl Johans Gatan in the center of Trondheim is one of our favourites in Norway. We keep bumping into Jørgen, the manager and co-owner, when we travel around the world. We met him in New York and went to "Blacktails" and "Attaboy" together when we were there to visit Nicolas and all the others.

He is here tonight to let us in. The bar is closed and outside the snow is falling heavy and wet. The Atlantic mid-December cold runs through the streets. Lights blend with Christmas decorations and we got slightly lost on our way here, asked for directions and the girl was very helpful and her mom was pretty and we were covered in snow.

When we were here last, we got evicted from a Burger King for reasons. We laugh about that

and about Berlin Bar Show and the shenanigans that ensued and cocktails we drank together in New York and that crazy night first time we were here. We like Trondheim.

Opening in December 2010, Raus, meaning warm, welcoming, polite, hospitable in the local dialect, is a large-ish venue fitting about 150 people, a DJ and 6 bartenders and waiters on a Friday night. They are, apart from the DJs, an 8 man operation, 5 of those full time, which means you don't get to get sick and you don't get to get time off. Still they have hired only two new people in the last three years. They believe in treating staff like family, taking people on outings, basically being reasonable and providing a home away from home for the staff.

Management meets every Monday to compare notes on new cocktails and once a month the entire staff is invited to chip in. New cocktails are suggested here and then Jørgen will filter the input and create cocktails, which then get filtered back through the system, and in this reflux system, the menus evolve.

They often use akvavit and more and more so.

"Basically we started out substituting gin with taffel or dill and rum or whisky with dark akvavit, like making an akvavit sour on barrel aged akvavit. Then we went on to a more adaptive phase, where we would take classics and instead of fitting an akvavit into that recipe we would fit the recipe to the akvavit. And finally we started making cocktails with a base in akvavit, what does it want, where will it go?"

We follow that lead. Ask him about what it means to their way of making cocktails. He ponders a bit.

"We start with a base flavour. A basic expression. It might be a new syrup, or a spirit or a purée. Then we ask what the flavour wants... We taste things and then we make patterns, or libraries of notes, right? So later you taste something else and you find that note in the library and see what else pops up in that category."

It makes sense in its own way. We taste a rather large variation of drinks and decide that it is indeed a good way. We also drink some local beer and some that isn't local. It's cold outside and no-one wants to go out into it.

"But look what happens other places," he says, and pulls out Smuggler's Coves large book on Tiki cocktails and looks up the

Norwegian Paralysis

45 ml Linie Aquavit, 45 ml pineapple juice,
45 ml orange juice, 15 ml lemon juice, 7,5 ml orgeat,
7,5 ml muscovado syrup

"This was a real eye opener for me; it's so simple and still very complex. Akvavit is really good at all this soft and elegant stuff, but it can also do Tiki and that is really funny."

A DIFFERENT JOURNEY

45 ml Linie Aquavit
15 ml St Germain
20 ml lemon juice
20 ml simple syrup
3 slices of cucumber
3 dashes virgin forest pepper tincture

The akvavit gives it a deep herbaceous note while the pepper cuts through and gives length and warmth.

When it comes to the future of akvavit we quickly get to the topic of driving cocktails and the problem we have is that akvavit evolved in a region with a rather primitive approach to mixed drinks. "Kaffepunch" is basically akvavit and coffee, while the "Mælkedreng" [milk boy] is fresh cow's milk and some sort of brændevin [Scandinavian for burned wine]. In Norway there is the "Fjellbäk" [mountain creek], a highball consisting of a mix of akvavit and vodka, topped with clear lemonade like Sprite and a dash of Rose's Lime Cordial. Then there is the "modern Danish classic" from the 1970's, the "Flyversjus" [sjus means drink, flyver is an airplane]; another highball of taffel akvavit and artificially made lemon soda, which can be made interesting and has a good story, but on its own is neither globally reproducible, nor all that nice…

As we say our goodbyes and leave Jørgen and Raus, there is a string of words hanging like snowflakes around us. Slowly our journey is crystallising into an understanding that we need to explore how the category can develop an inherent cocktail culture, with roots in tradition and history, but also a culture that looks forward. Something that can earn akvavit its own place within a modern drinking culture. With this, and slightly dizzy from beers and drinks, we go into the dark and snow to try and find a way out.

SOME SORT OF MARTINI

50 ml pineapple mayweed Atlungstad taffel
10 ml Lillet Blanc
10 ml Dolin Dry

Stir and serve ungarnished
The cocktail was made as a pairing for a pepper crab dish at Credo, a very nice restaurant in town. It's a martini style cocktail using pineapple mayweed infused Atlungstad Taffel, an akvavit that pays homage to akvavits of yesteryear with a spirit cut on the heavier end containing bits of fusel, blended with hint of Lillet Blanc and dry vermouth.

No Stress

Bergen sits quietly in a nest of mountains on the Atlantic coast. The land looks torn and rugged as we fly in, but the wooden houses that make up the residential outskirts are almost soft to the touch and painted in joyful whites, dark reds and pale blues. The city centre is built in stone and looks rich and wealthy, with broad boulevards and majestic statues on every corner.

The cobbled side streets around the harbour, the still beating heart of the old Hansa city and until 1314 capital of the very early Norway, are filled with coffee roasters, bars, cafés and restaurants. We have very good and very black coffee served by laughing girls by an old granite church and then head over to No Stress to talk to Simon Selvik.

PEPPER CARROT SMASH

40 ml Lysholm no.52
1,5 cm red bell pepper
30 ml carrot juice
20 ml lemon juice
20 ml simple syrup

Shake well and strain into tumbler over ice. Like at Up&Up the bell pepper is an obvious partner for the akvavit. Savoury and straight forward.

No Stress is just one of many bars run by Simon and his partners. They have a slider restaurant called Vinyl, a night club called Parken and finally Vaskeriet [the laundromat] – a dancehall ping pong slush ice bar downtown. In total, they employ around 30 bartenders, with a variety of programs spanning from kegtails at Vinyl over bottled drinks at Parken to slushed chili Margaritas at Vaskeriet and plain weird fun at No Stress.

The bar is 5 years old, built in an old street wear shop called Stress that sold DJ vinyls and sneakers. For young kids like Simon and his friends it was a legendary place, and the street smart youngsters cried out in furious agony when the shop had to close. So they fought for three years to reopen it as a bar, but being young and untested, no one would give them the time of day. It wasn't until an investor came on board they were able to start refurbishing it and on the day before the official opening they bought out the investor and changed the program from cheap beers and shooters to a local cocktail dive. Three of the four owners are born and raised in the streets around the bar and quickly old friends and relatives started showing up. Today, five years later, they are as busy as ever, open a full 7 days a week.

The back bar has been expanded several times, as the assortment of bottles change with the team's fancies. Recently they have been stocking up on akvavit.

"We have an old fashioned made on Opland Edel [a 5 year old Akvavit matured in madeira casks] on the menu. It's called Ulf Fashioned because it was a regular called Ulf who demanded we stock Edel and use it for cocktails. So he can come here with his friends and order a round of drinks named after him. We like to work like that, it creates a bond with the guests and friends…"

He goes on to explain a classic and by now well-known problem for bartenders.

"I hated akvavit when I was younger. I brought vodka for family gatherings to put in the freezer next to the akvavit. We need hard liquor to wash down the salty fatty winter foods here, but I just wouldn't drink akvavit. But then one of my friends started making "Arvesølvet" [Family Silver – one of the few white akvavits in Norway] and pushed me to using it and suddenly I started thinking about the flavours we get from it, the heavy food, notes of caraway and dill and anise. And I realized it was great in cocktails, it was natural. Actually something like Falernum, the spice profile is very Caribbean, but in Scandinavia those spices are used for winter food, Christmas dinners and all that, and also vegetables, you know?"

He gets quite excited and trails off into talking about making cocktails from scratch, not bending or twisting classics, but starting all over from the start with a smell left over from a dream. We draw a natural line to earlier discussions and he agrees.

"If we are to make this category last, it sits on a burning platform and we need to make it sexy again, so if we are to do that we need to find a new canvas. We can't just make martinis, it isn't enough, that canvas is full. It's what we do here, we start from the bottom. We get raspberries from

AKVAVIT DAIQUIRI

40 ml white pepper and coriander seed infusedno52
30 ml lime juice
20 ml simple syrup

Shake well and double strain into cocktail glass. Spicy and warm with a distinct sweetness.

a farm up north, there is a cider house a bit to the south, work with what you have locally, you know? But also, the category itself needs to get sexy, Lysholm no52 (a white, so-called "botanical akvavit" that borrows its aesthetics from the artisanal gin category) is a great example, but it is also kind of an akvavit posing as a gin."

It isn't a bad thought. Maybe we can allow the category to spaz out a bit, maybe we need the sexy gin look-alikes, but maybe there is space as well for spirits made with wild caraway, pot stilled potato spirit, extremes.

Bergen is one of the rainiest places in Europe and most certainly the wettest place in Norway in many respects. On average, they get well over 2 meters of rain and snow every year, mostly rain due to the mild golf stream climate. For hundreds of years it was a problem to fill the bishop's seat because the populace was drunk as sailors. Which they incidentally were – sailors. The Hansa cities had a standing army of 2500 young men stationed here ready to sail out if a king should impose an unwanted tax and these soldier sailors drank. So spirit has always been a part of the city's legacy.

Today it takes the form of a somewhat more civilized drinking pattern. Young people will take their student grants and move to other countries to study. Norway is a very expensive country and the grant will simply last you longer in other countries, so Berlin, London and Paris are common places for students to go to. When they come back, Simon says, they've tasted the rainbow and 20 years ago they were simply fed up with the lack of choice in Bergen.

In 2001 Club Metro then opened. They imported a team of six bartenders from top bars in London, and for years it was the place in Scandinavia that ran through the most alcohol with a cocktail list of 80(!) cocktails from famous bars around the world.

You can argue the validity of the concept today, but for its time it was an important game changer in the city and today Bergen can showcase around 15 cocktail bars.

And tourists come here to take pictures of the narrow ancient streets and drink something local.

"They go crazy for akvavit cocktails. The locals are still somewhat hesitant, but tourists love it. I think we should push much harder for global distribution, we need bartenders who don't have that fear of akvavit to work with it. To see it for its exoticism, instead of us who see it covered in conservative tradition. At the same time in cocktail bars around Norway I see this taboo surrounding it, giving it this bad boy image, like, you know, you can't use that! Like tequila was ten years ago. So bartenders want to use it, it's a place where we have the element of surprise in the meeting with a guest."

Pigalle

Oslo is the capital of Norway. Just north east of the central station there is a smallish part of town called Grønland [Greenland] like the island. It is sort of a town within the city, has a quite distinct multi ethnic feel, Indian restaurants and Iranian green grocers interspersed with second hand clothes shops and brown bars with quiet faces in the light of early morning drinking.

In the midst of this is Pigalle. It's the upper floor of Olympen, a restaurant serving classic Norwegian and Swedish grub, in a room filled with chandeliers and leather upholstery. Pigalle is something else entirely. Art deco, wood panels, green marble and porcelain panthers. And in the middle of all that, until the spring of 2017 that is, Anne Maurseth.

Olympen deserves a special mention here. It was a communal gathering house for almost 100 years, with a loft for private dining. In the 70s that loft was refurbished as Pigalle, a notorious strip joint, while the downstairs went punk and pool bar. As Anne says it was where you went when no one else in town would serve you. When it was taken over in 2007 by a new group of owners, Pigalle was a rockabilly dance bar that was never open.

Anne finds akvavit interesting for its savoury palate, compared to many other spirits the flavour profile is very strong and pungent.

"You should go for vegetables more than exotic fruits when pairing. Carrot juice before orange juice. But then, the flavours in the Nordic kitchen are very mild, subtle, like birch sap, pine shoots, rowan berries, all those little gems, they are so mild, they can so easily disappear and it's just not my style in cocktails…" she pauses for a second or two, then finds the words. "I like to think of cocktails as chapters of a book: The book is your evening and every chapter should be memorable. But we don't really do mild and subtle here, we do fun and wild and surprising."

It's refreshing to see her pull forth yuzu wine and banana liqueurs and the irony isn't completely lost on her. "Just write that I believe bananas to be indigenous to Norway", she tells us, laughing.

We wonder how she got around to mixing banana liqueur and Akvavit and she doesn't stop laughing.

"I was up in the mountains hunting with a hunting party a while back, and … Do you have Twist in Denmark?" Twist is a brand of chocolates you buy in bags and the individual chocolates are wrapped in a twist of paper. They emulate flavours of known brands, everyone has their own favourite and you eat them when you visit your grandparents. There's always one type left in the end."

"It's always the banana that's left and I love them, I do, they are mine, but on the mountain, there was a guy who ate them and we were fighting over them. I tore the last one out of his hand and ate it real fast and took a sip of Gammel Opland akvavit and I thought to myself 'this is great!' And then it turned into a cocktail."

SAVE THE LAST TWIST FOR ME

40 ml Linie Aquavit Madeira Finish
15 ml lustau oloroso sherry
15 ml Boudier banana liqueur
3 dashes Bob's Chocolate Bitters

Stir and serve straight up, with a banana Twist chocolate.
The nutty oxydization from the sherry with the sweetness from the madeira barrel lay a deep bed for the fine banana and chocolate notes. Everything tied together by the caraway/anise profile of the core spirit.

> "The book is your evening and every chapter should be memorable."

So in its own way we stay with the old flavours, with the childhood comfort, with the history, while Anne keeps talking about the "new Nordic", the chefs and the foraging.

"I don't know, maybe it's just that we would rather be fun and surprising than conceptually sound. I understand and I respect the effort but we can't all... we just do something else. If you want to use all these soft mild flavours, well sometimes you just need to reinvent how to make a cocktail and it's really interesting, but we like our big flavours here at Pigalle."

AGURKNYT
[SILLY SEASON -ED:]

40 ml Lysholm no.52
20 ml yuzu-shu (fortified yuzu wine)
25 ml cucumber juice
30 ml lemon juice
20 ml simple syrup

Shake and serve on crushed ice with strips of fresh cucumber

Intro cocktail for people who think they don't like akvavit. Thirst quenching and sharp acidity, light bitterness from yuzu and light caraway from Lysholm no52.

DENMARK

SPRING 2017

Skt Pauls Apothek

Aarhus is the second largest city in Denmark. It sits just under Mols and is the home of just over a quarter of a million people making it the second largest city in Denmark. It traces its roots back to around 700AD and the name derives from the old norse Ārōs, meaning the mouth of the river. The more you know. Aros is now the name of the art museum in the center of town, which is a great place to visit.

    Hasse Bank Johansen is the co-owner of Gedulgt, a small speak easy style cocktail bar, as well as Skt Pauls Apothek. For this interview, we meet him at Skt Pauls in Jægergårdsgade, an old apothecary refurbished as a cocktail bar and restaurant in 2009. In the summer of 2015 he published his cocktail book (in Danish) and in the

fall of 2016 his line of bar gear hit supermarkets all over Denmark. We meet him for at talk about heritage and taking ownership of local produce.

Skt Pauls Apothek is a cocktail bar / restaurant, serving cocktails with food. Hasse and the rest of the bar team make sure the waiters treat the cocktail servings like wine, in the sense that all cocktails are served with a story and an explanation as to why it works with this specific food. The bartenders act more like chefs, with very little guest contact, which has an enormous impact on how people order.

90% of guests choose a set menu, 3-5 courses with cocktails. That means the guests do not get to pick and choose their cocktails. That, in turn, means that any cocktail on the menu is served routinely for almost everyone who enter.

"We work a lot with the texture of the cocktails. The menu and the order of the servings have to make sense. You can't serve 3 egg white heavy cocktails in a row. The textures have to change, and the base spirit should do the same. We try to incorporate akvavit on the menu as much as possible,

as well as Nordic produce. It isn't dogmatic, but we feel we have an obligation to keep the Nordic tradition alive here."

"We more or less stopped using fruit. It's too easy. You know, we need to make something that isn't too extreme, but on the other hand we want to give people an experience. It's like using vodka, it's easy to make something everyone can drink, but you don't get any depth or nuances. It's the same with fruit, who doesn't like strawberries, right? But why keep beating that horse? Instead we make reductions, like stout and marshmallow and my current favourite – apple vinegar gastric. It works like salt almost, just a bar spoon is enough to open up the flavour of a cocktail. We also make a seaweed decoct and an oolong tea reduction boiled for 4 hours with citric acid. We get the fruity notes from these vinegars and reductions instead and it's much heavier, much more complex."

The first cocktail Hasse makes is literally a foam. It's called White Sands after the place on the west coast of Jutland where his father is from.

HVIDE SANDE

3 cl of Gammel Opland akvavit
3 cl sea-buckthorn juice*
1 cl simple syrup
3 cl lemon juice

Add it all to a shaker with the white of an egg. Shake it well, then charge the chiffon with nitrogen, not co2. The cocktail is then shot into a marmalade jar and topped off with a dash of Qcumber cucumber soda

The akvavit is a slight touch in the foreground, then balances out with the buckthorn. The cucumber soda adds freshness. The whole serve is light and frothy like a Ramos Gin fizz, but without the creamy solidity.
*500 g sea-buckthorn, 500 ml water, 250 g sugar, bring to a simmer and blend. Filter through cloth and store refrigerated for up to a week. Served with mackerel, kale and mussel stock.

"You'll notice it's quite weak in alcohol, but we send our guests through a 3-5 cocktail flight and a champagne cocktail, so you can imagine what would happen if we served everything at full strength."

"The akvavit here is just a touch to underline the fruity wintery notes. It is really cool how akvavit can do both, it can be the backbone in a cocktail, it can give the full throttle but it can also be a modifier, a slight hint to add spices in the background."

They are in the process of reworking the next cocktail. It's supposed to be entered for the Danish Bartender championship later the same day, so they are in a bit of a hurry, and as we take pictures and chat, Bastian, the head bartender from Gedulgt, is adding and subtracting ingredients. The recipe showed here is how it appeared on the winter menu, although personally I think the addition of the Stout/marshmallow syrup was genius. "Don't add that", Hasse says, "it's too complicated, let's put something in there, people can make at home." Yes sir.

CHERRY DE VIE

1 egg yolk
3 cl Frederiksdal Cherry Wine 2015
1,5 cl Linie Aquavit Christmas Edition
0,5 cl lemon juice
1 cl simple syrup
3 cl mandarin juice
Dash of orange bitters

Shake and double strain into coupette.

Again, it is a fairly light cocktail alcohol wise, but it is heavy and rich. The Christmas edition of the Linie Aquavit is darkened by heavier botanicals and along with the crisp and tart cherry wine from Frederiksdal on Lolland and the egg yolk we get a dark and rich, yet strangely forthcoming and fresh cocktail.

Duck and Cover

Duck & Cover, owned and managed by Kasper Riewe Henriksen, opened in april 2013. The décor is early sixties Danish design.

The bar sports around 45-50 seats and only takes seating guests. As any bar with that policy it has taken some time to let potential guests understand the concept, but the neighbourhood has welcomed Kasper and his staff.

The last few years a lot of effort has gone into defining a personality, creating a house style, so to speak. The menu in the beginning was rather conservative, without being boring. It was a knife's edge to balance on, to on the one hand

have something that everyone likes, something people recognize, so when they come back with their friends they can point and say, "have this one" and on the other hand to keep it fresh and interesting. As time has passed in the bar and guests have come to know the style and what to expect, the style has progressed into a somewhat more playful tune.

Everyone is involved in creating new cocktails. There is a menu meeting every other month and bartenders, who double as floor staff, are invited to chip in. Kasper will set a task – make a martini, use this or that product, create something fresh. Sometimes they leave the meeting with a finished menu, other times more work is needed, but when everyone is constantly invited to create, they expand their horizon and become better bartenders, is Kasper's philosophy.

With the growing confidence guests have in the bar, a lot of the early challenges have been eradicated. Akvavit was, for instance, something people distrusted, but today tourists expect it and even locals have opened to the idea. But they do utilize another trick; in the descriptions in the menu, the actual spirit is often omitted and replaced with tasting notes.

"Take the Stress Reliever (see elsewhere) – if we write taffel akvavit in the description no one orders it, but it is one of the best-selling cocktails here and we never get returns."

"If we take akvavit it has a much more open starting point than say, rum or whisky. We might have approached it more

| AMBER & WINE | 4 nordguld
2 lillet blanc
1 bspn orange curacao | Stirred and served up with a quarter slice of lemon |

"If you always dress up as someone else, how is anyone supposed to get to know you?"

like gin in the beginning, but I feel we are far beyond that. It's about simplicity, and that is the most difficult thing, isn't it? We focus more on savoury notes these days, within the framework of 'Scandinavia'. Does it grow here, can I go find it in the back yard?" Kasper frowns a bit, looks out the window and sips his coffee. "We have a business to run here, right? We are very busy and it drains you. When you are drained and empty, you can't be creative. So how do we recharge? I recharge by getting excited, by doing something new, by

seeing something new work and make people happy. Can we dig deeper into the roots of the flavour, can we go new directions? That is exciting, that gives me energy, then we have fun and then we make money. It comes down to why I wanted to make my own bar. I wanted to make something else – a cosy… like a living room, see, even the bar here, we stand at the same level as the guests, it's a choice. To make a setting where people relax, where they don't need to feel underdressed or in the way or not worldly enough to be allowed to order. That was the goal and I think we are succeeding."

Kasper spent a few years doing work for Havana Club Denmark and have made his fair share of mojitos. For him akvavit came almost as a cultural calling.

"Rum was the thing bartenders talked about back in the days, triangular trade me this and molasses me that, but all the time, we kept looking for that authenticity, searching for that "true" thing and all the time we had akvavit just at our feet. It's fun to see how akvavit has gone beyond this fad phase and have become a thing that bartenders just use with that matter-of-fact-ness that gin and whisky has as well…"

And that leads Kasper to a sort of a closing. That akvavit needs to remember that it is akvavit. It isn't the tequila of the north, or "like a caraway gin", akvavit is akvavit, with all its rich and long history.

"If you always dress up as someone else, how is anyone supposed to get to know you?"

ACROSS THE EQUATOR

3 cl Linie Aquavit
3 cl sweet madeira
1 cl simple syrup
1 bspn absint

Stirred and served on the rock with salt spray and lemon zest

Ruby

In June 2007 Rasmus and Adeline Shepherd-Lomborg opened Ruby, with Nick Kobbernagel-Hovind as the daily manager. It is difficult to neglect the impact the bar would end up having on the Scandinavian cocktail scene. We sit down with old friend and former colleague to both of us, Nick Kobbernagel-Hovind. Today he functions as operational manager for the three bars: Ruby, Lidkoeb and Brønnum. But we meet at Ruby for the very simple reason that this was where everything started for us. This is where we sat in the early

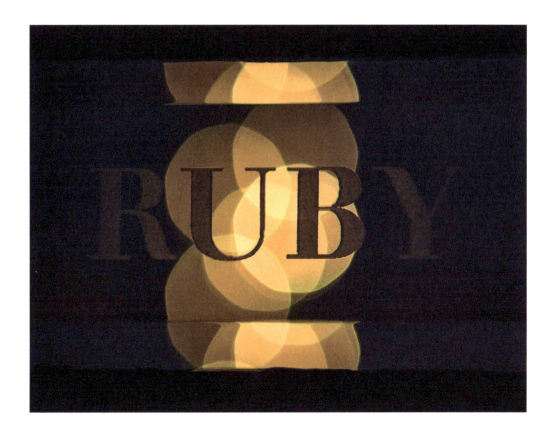

mornings after service and talked about Scandinavian bartending. This is where we had our first sips of akvavit while actually tasting it, instead of just washing it down. But Ruby wasn't about Nordic bartending in the beginning.

Nick recalls:

"We got quite a lot of attention internationally from the beginning. Adeline was the main reason for that, with her international profile having worked at highly decorated Oloroso and Bramble in Edinburgh."

There was a clear Noma effect, foodies came flocking to Copenhagen and all these tourists came after eating Michelin food and asked, "what is Danish, what do you drink?"

In the beginning there was no akvavit at Ruby. It came out of a very real fear that people would order it as shots and there was a clear intention to not be a shot bar. For slightly similar reasons there was no Bacardi and no Bombay Sapphire. Not a matter of taste, but simply a matter of forcing people to think before they ordered.

Then one summer there arose a need for a fresh cocktail on light spirit and Nick was looking for inspiration. And there, in the supplier's catalogue, under vodka, akvavit was listed.

On a Side Note

Ruby is placed in an old townhouse from 1740 in the oldest part of town, facing the parliament buildings and Thorvaldsen's museum. The building has been used for many purposes during the years; everything from a book press to private bank and even part of the cultural ministry. Most important to our history is the fact that De Danske Spritfabrikker (the Danish Spirit Factories – Ed:) had their headquarters here in the early years after their formation in 1881. Between 1882 and 1891, legendary akvavit characters C. A. Olesen and Isidor Henius had their offices here.

GREEN & WHITE

2 cl White chocolate Cream (250 g white chocolate dissolved in 1 litre cream at 45°C)
3 cl Den Ny Spritfabrik Argentum (dill akvavit)
3 cl Creme de cacao (clear)

Shake well, but short. Double strain into coupette and grate root of liquorice on top.

The cocktail is built on an alexander but goes quite far beyond. The white chocolate with the dill was a given when Nick tasted the akvavit first. Liquorice and white chocolate has been a Copenhagen dessert classic for years.

Today we laugh about that a good deal, symptomatic as it was for the general attitude towards akvavit. But one thing led to another and the "Jubilee Sour" was born, a fresh little thing with Aalborg Jubilæumsakvavit and calvados, cardamom and coriander leaves. It was an instant hit.

Then "866" came along, a funny dill/Campari/pink grapefruit thing with a salt rim on the glass.

Then Iceland Air made a double fold article on akvavit cocktails and things picked up.

"One day we got invited to come and speak at Manhattan Cocktail Classics. We discussed back and forth and didn't want to go and do the same old 'this is our bar and this is what we do', so we ended up deciding to do something about akvavit. And that is when we realized we didn't know anything about it. I even remember Rasmus (Poulsgaard – Ed:) saying 'I do not think I have ever truly *tasted* an akvavit'".

As Lidkoeb opened in '14 the Nordic profile was an integrated part of the house. The new bartenders got so caught up in the mood that Nick remembers it as right out difficult to get them to do cocktails *without* akvavit in them, but then again, it makes perfect sense for the house, as Lidkoeb is housed in an old apothecary and "lidkøb" is something you drink to seal a trade, like a handshake or a contract. In this instance a glass of akvavit or brændevin.

"It's like they didn't even think it was weird, it was just natural for them, the young bartenders. We had to overcome all that stigma and the young bartenders they just pick it up and roll with it, isn't that amazing?"

"Akvavit", says Nick, "deserves its place in a back bar. It goes from soft and mild O.P. Anderson to the sweet dark-

ness of Gilde Non Plus Ultra, it spans so wide and can handle almost anything you throw at it – I've never tried using it and thinking 'well, that certainly didn't work with akvavit' and that's the beauty of it. It's so versatile, but you are never in doubt if it's akvavit, it's always there, always present."

There is a very distinct way of constructing cocktails at Ruby. It's a sort of a finger print that makes sure that guests always know where they are. The finger print has of course changed over time, but the essence is intact.

"Nothing is ever shut down or closed, everything is kept open. Inspiration comes from everywhere, dinner or a song or a walk with the kids or a chef talking. Sometimes we take out cocktails from years ago and brush them off, sometimes it's just a note, like 'pistachio and grappa' scribbled somewhere. But we always start with a spirit, analyze it, find the key notes, establish a landscape. Then build on that. That's how we make sure the spirit is always first in the cocktail.

In the first couple of years the menu was fairly classic and rather fruity. But we have evolved and so have the guests. Today we can present much bolder flavour images, the guests are much more adventurous and so are we."

DEN HVIDE GREVE
(THE WHITE COUNT)

3,5 cl Aalborg Nordguld Akvavit
2,5 cl Gran Classico Amaro
3 cl Cocchi Americano
Thyme and lemon zest

Stir on ice and strain into tumbler full of ice. Garnish with lemon zest and thyme. Strong, spirit forward, with a wonderful bitterness on the aftertaste that lingers on. It is a Lidkoeb classic now, and a great example of how Aalborg Nordguld Akvavit bridges the gap between gin and aged spirits.

Mixing

a

navian

ide

Scandi
entity

We set out with a vague understanding of a project and came home with a much fuller picture. Half way through the journey we realised that there was a collective understanding of the category that, if documented and systemised, would turn into more than just a travel diary.

There was a clear need for driver cocktails – simple or refined – that could lift the category into bars and living rooms. Akvavit needed a rebranding, a break with 60 years of drinking culture – to be pulled out of the freezer and into a bar cabinet with the other real spirits. To be placed in a modern cocktail context, which would appeal to a younger drinking crowd.

Many of our discussions with bartenders revolved around the forming of a unique Nordic drinking identity. A new direction that looked inward rather than outward and which was built on tradition and cultural understanding of our culinary heritage, put into a modern context. We needed something that made sense on a deeper level. Something that would carry us forward and make drinking in Scandinavia interesting and different.

We need to dig deep into our roots. Scandinavia, to us, is a feeling more than anything else. Through all our mind maps and brainstorms, we found ourselves starting in flavours and tastes and ending in colours and emotions. The distinct Nordic light, the sound of a melancholic piano minor, slow moving candles, endless summer evenings.

We were, thus, faced with the challenge of discovering what and how a Scandinavian cocktail would taste and look like, using regional spirits, ingredients and techniques. But also, to make it fit into a modern setting, much like the new Nordic food revolution had done years earlier.

We tried to build a conceptual framework that would encompass the ideas and sentiments expressed by the bartenders. We do not claim to have reinvented the wheel or

"There was a clear need for driver cocktails that could lift the category into bars and living rooms."

that the techniques presented in the following chapter are supposed to be our inventions. But starting with the four Scandinavian words below, we have attempted to at least point out a direction, rooted in our culture.

Nærhed

Nærhed is a Danish word for proximity and presence. We should use produce available around us. Citrus fruits are not here, but acids from apples and vinegars are. Pineapples and mangos are gone, but wild berries and root vegetables are in.

Use what you have. The essence of the land and the climate is captured by the local produce and flows in the spirit of akvavit.

Æstetik

The aesthetic feeling of the Nordic countries is often described with words like simplicity, subtlety and stringency. It is minimalistic, understated, clean and transparent. When we look at design and architecture, we look at clean lines, simple materials, everyday objects made extraordinary.

We strongly feel that Nordic Cocktails should be about cutting to the bone and removing everything that isn't imperative in creating the flavour expression desired. We find this in cocktails with few ingredients, simplistically made and with an understated sense of beauty.

> "Scandinavia, to us, is a feeling more than anything else. Through all our mind maps and brainstorms, we found ourselves starting in flavours and tastes and ending in colours and emotions. The distinct Nordic light, the sound of a melancholic piano minor, slow moving candles, endless summer evenings."

Sæson

Time rolls as wheels and the seasons of the north are one of the most defining traits of the land and maybe the one that has the largest impact on our mind-set.

We want the cocktails to reflect the seasons of Scandinavia. Use regional produce when they are ready and at their best to get the best out of Scandinavia. Rejoice in the creative challenge of a long and harsh winter.

Arv

Arv is heritage. Fermentation, brining, smoking, pickling and cordial making are techniques that have been used for hundreds of years in Scandinavia. They are the pillars of our regional cuisine, as the inherent seasonal characteristics of the Nordic countries oscillate between abundance and scarcity.

Find meaningful connections between history, traditions and your craft. Old techniques make new flavours.

AKVAVIT AND FLAVOUR HARMONIES

Akvavit is a new category in a cocktail context for many bartenders and so a framework of flavour harmonies has not been established. Most people have an idea about what to mix with rum, with whisky and with gin. We want to take the time here to touch upon the flavour harmonies of akvavit to supply you with an understanding of how and why they can be paired to make new expressions, rooted in Scandinavian flora and fauna.

Whereas balance can be a very subjective thing formed by cultural factors and personal affinities, flavour harmonies on an aromatic level, setting aside personal dislikes, seem to adhere to a more universal set of rules. It is for example possible via gas spectrometric analysis which detects different flavour molecules of the subject, to predict flavour harmonies rather precisely; www.foodpairing.com is a website that uses this technique surprisingly well. Another way of predicting aromatic matches is looking at food dishes. Chefs all around the world have never been more creative in this regard, but also traditional and regional foods bear an abundance of fantastic combinations just waiting to be made into a cocktail.

Another way of approaching flavour harmonies – and one of the more surprising discoveries we made in our endeavour into the wonders of akvavit – was the notion that plants that were botanically related seemed to taste good together: a reworking of the old saying "if it grows together, it goes together". This can sound banal until you contemplate the practical implications of this for us as bartenders. Imagine using a botanical chart of families and species to predict what makes sense to put together in cocktails. That is what we did.

It was the question of why the combination of dill, caraway, fennel and anise at one point in history, seemingly rather randomly, had become the predominant flavour in akvavit that enticed our curiosity and made us dig deeper.

It seemed as if there had developed a consensus over time that using these botanicals made sense because of their flavour compatibility.

We found that these botanicals were related botanically and possessed a lot of the same flavour molecules. Caraway, dill, anis and fennel come from the same botanical family called Apiaceae or Umbelliferae, in English "flowering plants" (luckily, from a mixing point of view, the family is massive. It is the 16th largest of the plant families and contains well known plants like angelica, anise, carrot, celery, chervil, coriander, cumin, hemlock, lovage, parsley and parsnip.) Analysing the flavour compounds of this botanical family further we found that other botanical families such as Asteraceae (fx terragon) and Lamiaceae (fx basil and peppermint) seemed to contain an overlap in flavour molecules and therefore were prone to create flavour matches with akvavit in cocktails.

The primary common flavour molecules present in Apiaceae, Asteraceae and Lamiaceae are: Anethol (chervil, green and star anise, green basil, celery and fennel), r-carvone (mint), s-carvone (caraway), estragole (tarragon and apple), eugenol (Thai basil and cloves), apigenin (parsley) and menthol (fresh coriander, mint, root vegetables).

It is important to point out that flavour matching is by no means an exact science and that flavour molecules contained in different plants and fruits highly depend on the exact variety, the place of cultivation, time of harvest and other factors. Just because there is an overlap of flavour

"Botanical familiarity was a rather precise/accurate indicator in relation to harmonious flavour combinations"

molecules in two subjects they do not necessarily create a flavour harmony.

But as we started experimenting with flavour combinations, based on our method, we found that botanical familiarity was a rather accurate indicator in relation to harmonious flavour combinations and that you could predict those by studying botanical families. This realisation was a cornerstone in constructing the flavour map presented in this chapter. It is by no means exhaustive, but it can give you an idea about how to approach making original recipes with akvavit and as a tool for twisting cocktail recipes found in this book, or any of your beloved classics.

Drawing a flavour map exclusively with ingredients native to the nordics would make sense in the context of creating a nordic drinking identity. But this book is also an inspirational tool for bartenders abroad, so we include a wider spectrum of produce. Turn the page and start mixing.

FLAVOURMAP
AN INTRODUCTION TO MIXING WITH AKVAVITS

Akvavit Læsk

Every spirit needs a driver. Something simple that makes sense in its cultural context. Gin has its tonic, rum has its coke and lime, whisky has its soda.

This cocktail was one of the last we made: you could say it was the end of the project – to simplify things to a point where they almost implode.

It is rather versatile – use a lighter gastrique for a white akvavit and serve it in a highball, use a darker one for a barrel aged akvavit and serve it like a whisky and soda. Make your own soda in a siphon bottle or on your soda stream. The advanced version of this is exemplified by the Raspberry Taffel later in the book, but here is the Akvavit Læsk.

A measure of akvavit
Soda
Gastrique to taste

Serve in fitting glassware on plenty of ice. Garnish as you see fit.

An example

4 cl Aalborg Nordguld
2 cl homemade gastrique
Top with soda

Served in a highball, ungarnished.

GASTRIQUE

200g vinegar of your own choice
100g sugar

Caramelize sugar in a sauce pan, the darker the sugar, the darker the taste, but do not burn it. Add vinegar and boil until the caramel is dissolved and reduce about half. Try adding fruits or spices to the mix while reducing for added flavour. Check out the flavour map on page 192 for inspiration.

OLD TECHNIQUES FOR NEW COCKTAILS

Travelling back and looking inward can sound very ethereal, but can also be very concrete. For us it meant to rediscover old traditional techniques and find that you can create new flavours without the use of futuristic equipment and turning your prep kitchen into a laboratory. It was about cutting to the bone and creating a sound foundation to build on. In the following you will find five basic techniques that can serve as a starting point for your exploration of Nordic flavour combinations.

Cordials

The creation of cordials is also a way of preserving the wonderful flavours and nutrients of the summer. It is a way of enjoying and reminiscing the summer in colder times, but also in a second whipping up a wonderful libation over ice on the terrace.

In the Scandinavian region, we don't have "exotic" fruits such as pineapple and mangos, but we do have an abundance of berries, apples and pears that thrive in the colder climate of the Nordics.

It is almost like a collective memory for us up here: gathering berries in the fall and watching the 3-tier fruit juicer, we call it a Tutti Frutti, slowly drip fat warm juice out into a jug. Then watch as a grandmother dissolves sugar in it and see it lined up on shelves in the outhouse. If we were lucky there was a chilled glass of it in the afternoon sun, with ice cubes and a Superman comic. Then later in the year, when winter came over the hills and everything was covered in grey and white, we would sip warm elderberry toddy made from the cordial and watch the snow fall.

We are not quite sure, either of us, whether they poured alcohol into our cups as well as their own, though it would explain a lot of things, but it is a perfect accompaniment to the long, cold, and dark Scandinavian winters and as comforting as a blanket made of golden retrievers. Well, not literally of course......

The Tutti Frutti is a wonderful machine that makes juice from fruit by steaming it. Water vapor rises through a tube and condenses on the aluminium lid, then drops onto the fruit and slowly soaks it. The fruit juice falls through a sieve in the bottom and is collected, and then you can drain it through a pipe. If you can't get a Tutti Frutti, you can do the same by simmering the fruit with water until the juice is extracted, and then carefully pour the fruit mash into a cloth and let gravity do its thing.

Fruit juice made with warm extraction has a different flavour than centrifuged or slow juiced fruit. The flavours are more concentrated and jammy. With added sugar, the juice turns into a cordial that will store the smells of summer long into the darkness of winter.

Cordial – base recipe

500 ml heat extracted juice
250 g sugar of choice

Add the sugar while the liquid is still warm and dissolve. Store in a cool and dark place. Adjust the sugar according to the acidity of the fruit in question.

Toddy for 4 people

1 dl black currant cordial
3 dl water
2 dl Linie Aquavit
½ dl Arnbitter
2 tbsp. Honey
A few slices each of lemon and orange
A cinnamon stick
A star anise

Mix homemade black currant cordial, honey, bitter, spices and slices of fruit in a sauce pan. Bring to a simmer and remove from heat. Add Linie Aquavit. Serve in proper glassware and garnish with a lemon slice.

Fermentation

Fermentation is not a manmade phenomenon, things have been fermenting since the beginning of time even before humans or our predecessor populated the earth.

Fermentation is a metabolic process that converts sugar to acids, gases (mainly carbon dioxide) and sometimes alcohol. Fermentation breaks down nutrients that we were not otherwise able to digest and one could go on about the wonders of fermentation and its health benefits, but other books have been written by authors with much greater insights. We thoroughly recommend Sandor Katz book "The Art of Fermentation" for a more in depth exploration of the fermentation universe.

Fermentation, though not exclusive to the Nordics, have always been a part of our daily intake. Before the second industrial revolution it was one of the only ways to store and keep food for longer periods of time. And even before agriculture was widespread in Scandinavia, the hunter/gatherer culture were fermenting their prey which then could keep over the long scarce and otherwise lean winters of our region.

In Scandinavia, a lot of our traditional cuisine is fermented including the much-lamented Swedish "surströmning" which recently has become known as a YouTube gag reflex provoking sensation. We have a tradition for burying fish and meats and later dig them up and devouring them. The texture and flavour changes and is in many instances an acquired taste, but for us Scandinavians it is the most natural thing in the world and something we associate with holidays and family gatherings.

The great thing about fermentation is its inherit LO-FI nature. It is easy to do and adds interesting flavours and textures to your ingredients and cocktails, as almost any fruit and vegetable can ferment. Here we present a simple and fool proof method to get you started fermenting local fruits and vegetables all year round.

A straightforward way to get started fermenting is to first juice the vegetable or fruit used as nutrient. You can either use a slow juicer or a centrifugal juicer, however the centrifuge can activate an enzymic process that separates the solids from the juice in some fruits, which is why the slow juicer is a better alternative. But it works fine either way.

Then take a thoroughly rinsed 1,5 or 2 L (or larger) plastic bottle, like a soda bottle, and add the juice. It is important that the bottle is only filled ¾, as it needs some space to work and expand in. It is also important that you use a container in which the liquid has a low surface area, as the fermentation can be difficult to control otherwise. Plastic containers are much easier to use compared to glass bottles, as you can squeeze the bottle during the process to get a sense of how much it has carbonated.

Screw on the cap lightly and let it sit on your kitchen counter for 3-4 days until bubbles start appearing in the liquid. Then strain the content through a colander, transfer to fridge and let it ferment for 3 weeks or more.

As mentioned before this fermentation process releases carbon dioxide into the beverage and creates pressure in the bottle. It is therefore important that you keep an eye on the ferment during the process and release pressure if the plastic container looks like it is about to blow up. An effective way of avoiding this is by only screwing on the lid lightly, so it can release pressure when it builds up within the container. Notice that when the lid is fully closed the liquid becomes carbonised. It is powerful forces at work here, so you should take it seriously, but if you pay attention there is nothing to be afraid of.

Taste the beverage underway, as it transforms itself from a juicy sweet lightly carbonated libation, to a more winy, funky, bubbly and cider-like liquid. When you feel the fermentation is just right in your new product, you can easily stop the process by drinking it.

This process can be repeated all year round, using everything from early summer rhubarb to late summer cherries and root vegetables such as beet root and carrots during the winter. You can add herbs and flavourings to the juice. Use the flavour map for inspiration.

The beauty of using your own fermentation in a cocktail is that all the work is done by nature. Something and apple juice is a bland and boring serve, but the same thing and homemade fermented apple cider is suddenly alive and exciting.

Cocktail

This is basically a "Stone Fence" on dill akvavit. The cider sat in a fridge for 3 weeks and the fermented apples go extremely well with the light, green, fresh notes of dill from the Argentum akvavit.
    Depending on glass size, you might want to adjust the amount of spirit to cider.

4 cl Den Ny Spritfabrik Argentum dill akvavit
top with apple cider

Garnish with slices of fresh apples and leave the car keys with someone you trust.

Shrubs and Pickles

Vinegar is the transformation of wine, beer, cider or other fermented fruit juice that through a chemical process in which the inherent ethyl alcohol undergoes partial oxidation that results in the formation of acetaldehyde. The acetaldehyde is then converted into acetic acid which happens to be an effective natural preservative, as it lowers the PH level and thus creates a less bacteria friendly environment. Through pickling, vinegar is an integral part of Scandinavian cuisine and has served as a way of conserving food for the barren and cold Nordic winters for many generations and hundreds of years.
    Pickled herring is a national staple in especially Denmark and is something of an acquired taste as the raw herring is prepared only by marinating them in a pickle brine consisting of sugar, vinegar and herbs and spices. The texture of the fat herring is silky smooth and the salty, sweet and acidic brine creates a wonderful rich and balanced taste,

but for the non-initiated it can be something of a mouthful. However, the idea of using vinegar and sugar to build taste is something that can be directly translated into cocktails.

The acidity from the vinegar adds freshness, nerve, a vibrant tone and increases the flavour intensity of the elements it is added to. It also creates balance and serves as a counter weight to sweetness in your concoction and can therefore be used as a substitute for citrus.

The process of creating vinegar is an organic and on-going process and the end result depends on a long array of factors such as the mother/starter, the temperature, the specific nutrient and many others. If you want to make you own it is both very easy and extremely complicated and the internet is full of interesting recipes that you can play around with, creating you own unique acidic element to your cocktails. If not, you can easily buy decent quality vinegar these days and as with anything else quality does matter. That is not to say that you cannot make lovely potions from generic white wine vinegar, but obviously the flavours will be different.

In principle, you can pickle or make shrubs from pretty much anything from herbs over vegetables to fruits and creating cocktails with it is easy and surprisingly tasty. Once you get started we recommend you use the flavour map to find ideas for flavouring agents. Compared to citrus fruit juice, the taste of vinegar is less sensitive to heating and simmering the vinegar with herbs, fruits and/or spices is a good and fun way to add flavours to a cocktail.

Raspberry Shrub

800g of raspberries
300g of sugar
400ml water

Bring to boil in a sauce pan. Remove from heat and strain through a sieve to get rid of the kernels.

Add 400 ml clear cider vinegar and refrigerate.

Grab a highball glass, fill it with ice, add Taffel and shrub. Then fill with soda, stir well, and garnish to your heart's content.

Raspberry Taffel

4 cl Aalborg Taffel
4 cl Raspberry Shrub
10 cl Soda

Salt

Curing or brining is a method that has been used for preserving meats and vegetables for as long as we have had salt. The most basic method is to cover something in salt and dig it out when you need it. After the treatment, it will keep almost indefinitely at outhouse temperature.
Traditionally in Scandinavia, fishermen would bury fish in sand above the tide line in a bed of salt, sugar and herbs, dill often being part of that mix. When you leave the fish there for a while, the salt extracts liquid from the fish and conserves it by creating an environment very hostile for the growth of spoilage bacteria.

We are not blessed with exotic spices in Scandinavia, but we do have salt everywhere. It flows in our veins and runs in our hair when we come home from the beaches. The massive fishing fleet in Scandinavia in the middle ages exported herring and cod to southern Europe, all preserved in salt. The mineral has historically been a dominant flavour in Scandinavian cooking. Of course we will utilize it.

So please add salt to cocktails, it opens aromas and adds wonderful complexity. This cocktail was created by Toke Christensen at Lidkoeb back in 2015. It's a tribute to the salt sprayed coast lines and the part of the North Sea that we call Vesterhavet – the west sea. (Look at a map of the North Sea, and find Denmark, then it makes sense.) Amber has a distinct pine flavour and the bitter contains anise and cinnamon, which, as you can see on the flavour map, works well with akvavit.

Vesterhavs Old Fashioned

1 bspn arnbitter (Danish stomach bitter)
2 cl amber liqueur
4 cl Barrel aged taffel akvavit (they made it at the bar)

Serve in tumbler on frozen pebbles with sea weed baked with rape seed oil and salt. Spray with saline solution (salt dissolved in water).

Dairy

Scandinavia has a love affair with dairy products. There it is, it is out there. We love everything from butter to cheese, milk and yoghurt. The agricultural sector is a huge part of Scandinavian economy and identity.

Every culture and part of the world have a distinct smell that you associate with them. You only notice it when the smell is unfamiliar, so we don't think about this ourselves, but some foreigners pick up a distinct scent of dairy like sour milk or yoghurt when "smelling us". So apparently dairy is oozing out our pores. It was the nomadic people who wandered in from the Caucasian wasteland after the ice receded that brought with them the ability to drink milk as adults, which is not common in large parts of the world. It would turn out to be a very helpful trait in the long cold winters and to this day we indulge in an excessive consumption of dairy products.

Most of us know cream and condensed milk in cocktail contexts, but other dairies such as butter milk, caramelized brown whey cheese and sour cream can easily be used in cocktails and creates a totally different texture, flavour and taste balance. And for cocktail purposes dairy has a funny build-in mechanism; it curdles. The protein in cow's milk is 80% casein, which is a phosphoprotein encased in a membrane. This membrane is susceptible to breaking when subjected to a sufficiently acidic environment. When it breaks, the casein will bundle in large lumps. These have a lot of purposes, cheese being one of them. The rest, the whey, is often discarded or used for animal fodder, but in a curdled or clarified milk punch it adds a silky smoothness.

In the summer time, we Danes like to mix buttermilk with egg yolks whipped frothy with sugar and call it koldskål (cold bowl). A dash of vanilla goes in there and fresh fruit and a small biscuit called "kammerjunker". We wanted to make something out of that, but you can't just make koldskål and call it a cocktail.

Buttermilk has a very distinct acidity from lactic acid and a wonderful creaminess. It curdles if you as much as look at it sternly. We can clarify it completely in minutes, which makes it much more useful for our purpose than full milk or half and half. We added a pinch of sea salt and brought it to a simmer, then let it cool slightly and poured it through a cloth.

A rhubarb cordial – made by dissolving 125g of white sugar in 250ml rhubarb juice from the Tutti Frutti – adds fruitiness. In Scandinavia, we often use a product called non-oxal. It is a chalk binding agent that saturates the oxal-

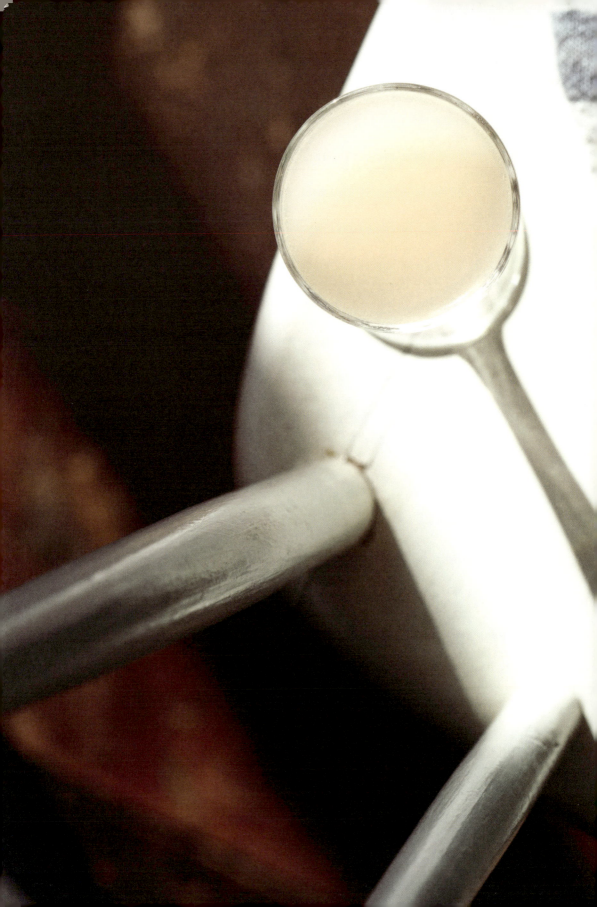

ic acid in rhubarb so it doesn't draw calcium from the body, but with the addition of a dairy product, even curdled, this is not necessary and as it does horrors to the colour making it milky white and sad, we don't recommend it.

Kammerjunker-infused Hammer Ulagret. The small cake/biscuit consist of butter, vanilla and sugar held together by a splash of flour. It dissolves quite readily in liquids. We poured it into Hammer Ulagret, an unaged Norwegian citrus forward akvavit, let it sit for 2 hours and filtered it. It is shockingly good on its own.

Now mix the three components in equal parts with another part of water. Chill and serve in small cups in the evening sun. If you add sparkling water instead of still water it gets fizzy and fresh. We do not totally agree whether this is a good thing or not.

A whey to get drunk (yes, haha, we are funny)

250 ml homemade rhubarb cordial
250 ml freshly made salted butter milk whey
250 ml kammerjunker akvavit
250 ml water – still or sparkling

Mix, chill and serve.

The kammerjunker akvavit adds vanilla, the rhubarb is for fruit and the buttermilk adds acidity. Use the flavour map to replace elements and make your own Scandinavolous milk punch.

That's all folks

We have spent over a year on this project. We have met with producers and akvavit aficionados, we have travelled the world and met bartenders and drunk their cocktails. We experienced a common passion for using akvavit as an ingredient in drinks, even though the approach was very different. In USA and England it was more of a novelty and something that could add an interesting flavour to their cocktail, which they couldn't get anywhere else. In the Scandinavian countries, akvavit is, as we have explained, deeply ingrained in our cultural roots, for better or worse.

But where do we take our craft in a world where most of us know how to make an Old Fashioned, a Gin Fizz or a Manhattan? We see the constant push from marketing executives, big corporations and opinion leaders to make cocktails ever more elaborate with more and more outlandish ingredients, garnishes and techniques. But is that the only way?

No of course not! Maybe it is time to slow down and reflect. What makes sense for you in the time and place that you live in – bearing in mind your personality and style?

Akvavit is a wondrous and wonderful spirit. We dearly want to save it from extinction and we absolutely believe that introducing it in modern cocktail culture is an important part of that. But this is much more than an akvavit project, this is a humane project. It is about finding yourself through your profession wherever that might lead you.

This project challenged us to think differently and, in a way, rethink how we thought of cocktails. It was a difficult process that involved self-criticism and reflection and is by no means over. It was a revolt against what we thought we knew and in a way a relearning altogether, but we got high from the enthusiasm expressed by the bartenders and our discussions on forming a unique Nordic cocktail culture in which bartenders could express their own heritage, traditions and creativity through cocktails. It was something that made sense for us on so many levels and something that is universally applicable depending on your cultural background.

The last chapter presents simple methods and recipes that we feel tell a story about where we are. We feel that through simplicity, transparency and honesty, we can make drinks and bars that guests truly enjoy themselves in – unintimidating and welcoming. We believe that beauty lies in simplicity. There is nothing more difficult than creating a simple drink, which solely relies on the combination of one or two flavouring agents and an alcohol that together elevate the whole. In this space, you are naked and vulnerable, there is no veil of confusion and pretence.

So this was our naked and vulnerable attempt to tell a story about our beloved Nordic spirit. You are more than welcome to reach out to us, if you want to tell your story with akvavit or have questions or answers. We have both.

AKVAVIT
Rediscovering a Nordic Spirit

Text and editing: Sune Urth and
Rasmus Poulsgaard
Design and layout: Bjørn Ortmann
Photos: Rasmus Poulsgaard
Illustrations: Matilde Digmann
Proof reading: William Bjarnø
Typeface: Founders Grotesk and
Founders Grotesk Text
Printed by: Narayana Press, Denmark

© 2017 Two Guys Publishing
All rights reserved. No part of this publication
may be reproduced or transmitted in
any form or by any means, electronic or
mechanical, including photocopy, recording
or any informational storage and retrieval
system, without prior permission from the
publisher

ISBN: 978-87-999974-0-4